AA

ORDNANCE SU
LEISURE GUID

BRECON BEACONS
AND MID WALES

Produced jointly by the Publishing Division of the
Automobile Association and the Ordnance Survey

Cover: Craig Goch Reservoir in the Elan Valley
Title page: high in the Brecons near Pen y Fan
Opposite: Crickhowell's medieval bridge spanning the Usk
Introductory page: the ancient church tower of Knighton, on the Welsh border

Editorial contributors: Chris Barber (Walks);
William Condry (A Variety of Wildlife);
Audrey Doughty (Gazetteer and Taking the Waters);
Dr J Geraint Jenkins (Sheep Farming and Rural
Occupations); Richard G Keen (Traces of Industry);
Jean Kingdon (Directory); Roger Thomas (History of
the Hills and Looking at the Landscape)

Original photography: Colin and Andrew Molyneux

Typeset by Avonset, Midsomer Norton, Bath
Printed in Great Britain by Chorley & Pickersgill Ltd,
Leeds

Maps extracted from the Ordnance Survey's 1:625 000
Routeplanner Map, 1:250 000 Routemaster Series
enlarged to 1:200 000 and 1:25 000 Pathfinder and
Outdoor Leisure Map Series with the permission of Her
Majesty's Stationery Office. Crown Copyright reserved.

Additions to the maps by the Cartographic Department
of The Automobile Association and the
Ordnance Survey.

Produced by the Publishing Division of
The Automobile Association.

Distributed in the United Kingdom by the Ordnance
Survey, Southampton, and the Publishing Division of
The Automobile Association, Fanum House,
Basingstoke, Hampshire RG21 2EA.

The contents of this publication are believed correct at
the time of printing. Nevertheless, the Publishers cannot
accept responsibility for errors or omissions, or for
changes in details given.

AA ISBN 0 86145 819 2 (Hardback)
AA ISBN 0 86145 800 1 (Softback)
OS ISBN 0 31900 52 (Hardback)
OS ISBN 0 31900 44 (Softback)

Published by The Automobile Association and the
Ordnance Survey.

AA reference: 12179 (Hardback)
AA reference: 10935 (Softback)

BRECON BEACONS
AND MID WALES

Contents

Looking at the Landscape 6

A Variety of Wildlife 10

History of the Hills 14

Traces of Industry 19

Taking the Waters 24

Sheep Farming 28

Rural Occupations 32

A to Z Gazetteer 36

Directory 73

Atlas Legend 82 / Atlas 86

Motor Tours 94

Walks 102

Index 118

Using this Book

The entries in the Gazetteer have been carefully selected although for reasons of space it has not been possible to include every community in the region. A number of small villages are described under the entry for a larger neighbour, and these can be found in the index. Variations in the usage of English and Welsh and in regional spellings may occur. A Welsh glossary appears on p73.

Each entry in the A to Z Gazetteer has the atlas page number on which the place can be found and its National Grid reference included under the heading. An explanation of how to use the National Grid is given on page 82.

Beneath many of the entries in the Gazetteer are listed AA-recommended hotels, restaurants, garages, guesthouses, campsites and self-catering accommodation in the immediate vicinity of the place described.

For reasons of space the AA-recommended establishments under some entries are a selection only. For full details see the AA range of annual guides and the AA *Members' Handbook*.

HOTELS

1-star	Good hotels and inns, generally of small scale and with acceptable facilities and furnishing.
2-star	Hotels offering a higher standard of accommodation, with some private bathrooms/showers; lavatories on all floors; wider choice of food.
3-star	Well-appointed hotels; a good proportion of bedrooms with private bathrooms/showers.
4-star	Exceptionally well-appointed hotels offering a high standard of comfort and service, the majority of bedrooms should have private bathrooms/showers.
5-star	Luxury hotels offering the highest international standards.
Country House Hotel (CH)	A hotel where a relaxed informal atmosphere prevails. Some of the facilities may differ from those at urban hotels of the same classification.

RESTAURANTS

1-fork	Modest but good restaurant.
2-fork	Restaurant offering a higher standard of comfort than above.
3-fork	Well-appointed restaurant.
4-fork	Exceptionally well-appointed restaurant.
5-fork	Luxury restaurant.
1-rosette	Hotel or restaurant where the cuisine is considered to be of a higher standard than is expected in an establishment within its classification.
2-rosette	Hotel or restaurant offering very much above average food, irrespective of the classification.
3-rosette	Hotel or restaurant offering outstanding food, irrespective of classification.

GUESTHOUSES

These are different from, but not necessarily inferior to, AA-appointed hotels, and they offer an alternative for those who prefer inexpensive and not too elaborate accommodation. Each establishment must usually offer at least six bedrooms, and there should be a general bathroom and a general toilet for every six bedrooms without private facilities.

SELF CATERING

These establishments, which are all inspected on a regular basis, have to meet minimum standards in accommodation, furniture, fixtures and fittings, services and linen.

CAMPSITES

1-pennant	Site licence; 10% of pitches for touring units; site density not more than 30 per acre; 2 separate toilets for each sex per 30 pitches; good quality tapwater; efficient waste disposal; regular cleaning of ablutions block; fire precautions; well-drained ground.
2-pennant	All one-pennant facilities plus: 2 washbasins with hot and cold water for each sex per 30 pitches in separate washrooms; warden available at certain times of the day.
3-pennant	All two-pennant facilities plus: one shower or bath for each sex per 30 pitches, with hot and cold water; electric shaver points and mirrors; all-night lighting of toilet blocks; deep sinks for washing clothes; facilities for buying milk, bread and gas; warden in attendance by day, on call by night.
4-pennant	All three-pennant facilities plus: a higher degree of organisation than one–three-pennant sites; attention to landscaping; reception office; late-arrivals enclosure; first-aid hut; shop; routes to essential facilities lit after dark; play area; bad weather shelter; hard standing for touring vans.
5-pennant	A comprehensive range of services and equipment; careful landscaping; automatic laundry; public telephone; indoor play facilities for children; extra facilities for recreation; warden in attendance 24 hours per day.

WALKS

The walks in this book have been carefully planned to suit families, but a few need particular care. Potential hazards are highlighted in the text. It is always advisable to go well-equipped with suitable clothing and refreshment, and, as an extra precaution, a compass.

BRECON BEACONS
AND MID WALES

Introduction

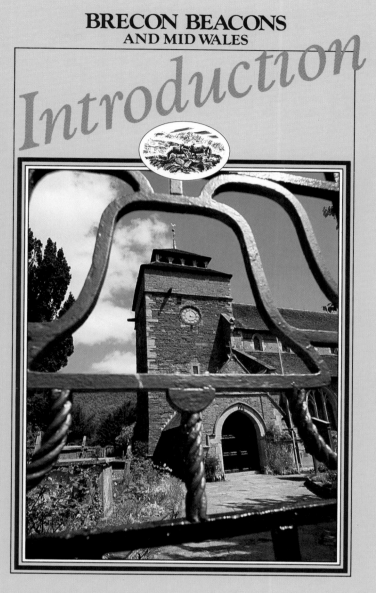

The area covered by this book is an enchanting combination of beautiful, varied scenery and a wealth of fascinating man-made legacies ranging from Roman forts to Victorian spa towns.

All the different elements that make this part of Wales so special are included in the book, and there is comprehensive coverage of where to go, what to see and do and where to stay.

Written by people who know and love the area and backed by the expertise of the AA and the Ordnance Survey, this attractive and authoritative guide will help you get the best out of this lovely part of Britain.

Looking at the Landscape

If there is one overall characteristic which dominates the landscape of this region, it is altitude. The area is filled with the uplands of South and Central Wales – the Brecon Beacons, Mynydd Eppynt, the Cambrian Mountains and Plynlimon. These are Wales's heartlands, a high country of moors, plateaux, forests and hill-sheep farmlands dissected by innumerable rivers and streams.

The height here has a resilience and consistency lacking in the up-and-down volcanic jumble of North Wales, a region of severe slopes, steep mountainsides and abrupt landforms. The height here is disguised. Unlike Snowdonia, there are no

great accelerations or reversals of scale. Consistency of height – much of it over 2,000ft – hides the true nature of these mountains. The gradual inclines and apparent gentleness of the slopes rob South and Central Wales's mountains of the grandeur shown by pinnacles such as Snowdon.

Dangerous ground

On a balmy summer's day, the flat-topped summit of Pen y Fan in the central Beacons, at 2,907ft the highest point in South Wales, can look positively benign. Its grassy flanks, extending upwards from the roadside in a far from breathless fashion, have nothing of the intimidating aura which hangs around the near-vertical slabs along Snowdonia's awesome Llanberis Pass, for example. Similarly, the wispy, boggy highlands of Plynlimon, east of Aberystwyth, can, on the rare days when the mists give way to clear blue skies, take on the appearance of a vast, grassy, petrified sea, its waves heaving gently towards an unbroken horizon.

But appearances can be deceptive. These uplands are mountains in every sense of the word. Conditions above 1,500ft can change alarmingly quickly, and danger is exacerbated by lack of shelter on the high, treeless, exposed moors, where it is easy to lose all sense of direction. The memorial to little Tommy Jones near Pen y Fan (see page 63) reminds visitors of just one of the victims of an upland range that has even claimed well-equipped soldiers on mountain exercise.

A geological overview of this region reveals a northern area blanketed by rocks of the Silurian period (though Plynlimon itself is an outcrop of earlier Ordovician rocks). This produces the characteristic upland scenery of gently undulating

The high moorland of the Black Mountains extends from Hay to the Sugar Loaf above Abergavenny

The vast reservoir of Llyn Brianne, opened in 1973, boosts the water supply of Swansea

Old Red Sandstone rocks stretch over 50 miles from the beautiful valley of the River Tywi

moorlands, peaty and acidic, boggy and shaly, rising to over 2,000ft and sliced through by deep river valleys.

This tough, unproductive and unforgiving highland produced an especially hardy strain of sheep farmer. The lonely, whitewashed stone cottages – sadly now all too often abandoned – scattered across these moors are enough to shatter any romantic view of farming on this marginal terrain. A drive across the haunting 'roof of Wales' on the old drovers' road between Tregaron and Abergwesyn brings home the realities. Young conifers sprout from rough, barren land where hill-sheep farmers once eked a precarious living, and its unyielding character is perfectly captured in this description of 1599: 'The air thereof is sharp and cold . . . the soil is hungry, rough and churlish and hardly bettered by painful labour.'

The National Park
The region's southern uplands are dominated by the Brecon Beacons National Park, a swathe of high ground moulded by the elements of Old Red Sandstone. The Silurian rocks to the north here give way to rocks of the less ancient Devonian period, the sandstones which produce that thick, glutinous red mud which adheres to country paths and roads (and walkers' boots!) throughout the Beacons.

The Brecon Beacons are perhaps the most misunderstood mountains in Wales. The problem largely lies in the names. The Brecon Beacons, after

which the National Park is named, are only one of four distinct mountain ranges within the park's 519sq miles. To confuse matters even further, two of the four ranges share almost the same name! Beginning in the east, and straddling the Wales/England border, we have the Black Mountains. Next come the central Brecon Beacons, followed by Fforest Fawr, an unbroken stretch of grassy, treeless hills. The far west of the park is filled with the brooding, forbidding empty wilderness of the Black Mountain (singular).

In South and Central Wales, these mountains inevitably capture the lion's share of attention because of their National Park status. But even without the National Park's stamp of approval, their landforms would still attract the majority of visitors, for the Brecon Beacons are where geography and geology leave the dull pages of the text book and assume an unforgettable reality.

Gentle rock
Old Red Sandstone is dominant throughout the Brecon Beacons Park. This softish rock weathers to create the classic Beacons landscape of rounded outlines, gradual gradients and mountains of harmonious uniformity languishing beneath big skies. The only real surprise comes when the southern slopes, after rising in gentle increments, suddenly plunge down a steep, north-facing escarpment.

These mountains as they now stand have been fashioned by the passage of glaciers. Stand on a ridge in the central Beacons and you will see how the great ice sheets ground their way across the landscape, smoothing out all irregularities in their path. Valleys which were once V-shaped have been scooped into a wide U-shape. Climb to the summit of Pen y Fan, or Fan Brycheiniog in the Black Mountain, and you will see how the passage of ice sheets has created cwms and glacial lakes. The waters of Llyn Cwm Llwch, a perfect little circular

lake beneath Pen y Fan, fill a basin scooped out by ice, while the Black Mountain's myth-laden twin lakes of Llyn y Fan Fach and Llyn y Fan Fawr were created when water collected behind debris left in front of melting glaciers.

Waterfall country

The only deviation from the Beacons' ubiquitous sandstones lies along the southern boundary to the park, where outcropping limestone, accompanied by bands of millstone grit, have created a distinctive environment characterised by craggy, wooded gorges, caves, pot holes and waterfalls. This complex landform is at its best just south of the village of Ystradfellte, in the 'waterfall country' of the Mellte, Hepste and Neath rivers. The Mellte tumbles down a series of spectacular falls downstream of Ystradfellte, whilst the Hepste boasts the most famous waterfall of all, Sgwd yr Eira ('The Spout of Snow') which overhangs to such an extent that walkers can follow a path behind its curtain of water without getting wet.

Waterfalls are by no means the only feature produced by the action of water on limestone. This soluble rock has eroded to form a labyrinthine underworld of fissures, pot holes and cave systems. Every last drop of the River Mellte, for example, is swallowed up by the giant, gaping mouth of Porth yr ogof near Ystradfellte, probably the largest cave entrance in Wales. Near the headwaters of the Neath, the river suddenly spills into a deep fissure known as Cwm Pwll-y-Rhyd. The convoluted effects created by water and limestone are even on view to the public, at the Dan-yr-Ogof Showcaves, where weirdly shaped stalactites and stalagmites can be seen, on guided tours of a vast cave system.

Rivers and lakes

Water is an element which has had a profound effect not only in the Beacons but throughout Mid Wales. Stories of the wet Welsh weather, although sometimes apocryphal, have a certain ring of truth when applied to the hills and mountains of Central Wales. High rainfall figures (up to 100in a year on

As soon as the Mellte meets the millstone grit sandstones, it begins a flight of lovely waterfalls

the higher ground) have produced sodden moors, countless streams and rivers, bogs and lakes. And man has imitated nature by constructing huge reservoirs to take advantage of guaranteed rainfall on poor, unproductive land.

The Elan Valley reservoirs, built around the turn of the century, were the first of a series of man-made lakes. These have since been joined by the inky-black waters of Nant-y-moch above Aberystwyth, spectacular Llyn Clywedog near Llanidloes and, most memorable of all, Llyn Brianne in the previously inaccessible hills north of Llandovery, creating a collective indentity as the Mid Wales 'lakelands'.

The Brecon Beacons Park also has its fair share of reservoirs, mainly around the southern slopes of the central Beacons. The park also contains, at Llangorse, the largest natural lake in South Wales, its waters and reedy shoreline an important habitat for flora and fauna but threatened, alas, by heavy recreational use and pollution.

Rivers are another important landscape feature. The consistent height of the mountains and plateaux is interrupted only when deep valleys have been created by running water. The sources of two famous rivers, the scenic Wye and stately Severn, are only a handful of miles from each other on a remote tract of hill and forest near Llyn Clywedog. A third major river, the Usk, has a particularly significant effect on the Beacons' landscape as it flows east and south-eastwards through a wide, sheltered vale.

The most celebrated river feature of all must be the 'dread chasm' (William Wordsworth's florid description) at Devil's Bridge, where the Mynach plunges 300ft in a series of torrents through a wooded, rocky defile on the way to its confluence with the River Rheidol. The shady, claustrophobic chasm, accessible by a near-vertical flight of steps, is perhaps the perfect antidote to the wide, open spaces and endless vistas of the Brecon Beacons.

A Variety of Wildlife

A voluntary Watch Committee, formed by the inhabitants of the Tywi Valley, recently saved the red kite from destruction at the hands of the egg collectors

At first sight the Mid Wales uplands present a harsh and hostile environment. To the north, Plynlimon has a heavy annual rainfall and is prone to turn into a huge peaty sponge. This boggy surface, stretching south across the moorlands and over the Brecon Beacons National Park, forms the greatest spread of peat in Wales; and to the west, Plynlimon's summit breaks into high crags, horseshoed around a corrie lake. But appearances can be deceptive, and the Mid Wales area is, in fact, rich in its variety of rare and fascinating wildlife.

Mountain rarities

On the western heights of Plynlimon, which stands 2,468ft above sea level, a few true mountain plants can be found: starry saxifrage, mossy saxifrage and dwarf willow all flourish here.

The sheep-grazed uplands from Plynlimon to the Beacons are vital feeding places for several rare British birds. There are probably more ravens on the uplands of Mid Wales than anywhere else in the country, and carrion sheep are an important part of their diet. Buzzards are also plentiful here, and there are occasional hen harriers, merlins and short-eared owls. The graceful and colourful red kite, which in Britain is confined to Wales, feeds mainly on the western moors of Mid Wales; and the upland bogs have communities of dunlins and golden plovers, here close to the southern edge of their breeding range.

The high moors of Mid Wales are an expansive

The Brecon Beacons boast a widely varied wildlife: the raven (above) patrols sheep country looking for carrion; purple saxifrage (top right) loves the rich lime of the local Old Red Sandstone; and roseroot (bottom right) is a member of the stonecrop family, named for its habit of clinging to rocks and stones

spread of hardy grasses, sedges and mosses; but there is less heather here, and fewer red grouse, than in the mountains and moors of North Wales. On the lower ground a few miry areas support a much richer wildlife: Rhos Goch Common, north of Hay-on-Wye, Cors y Llyn, south of Newbridge-on-Wye, and Tregaron Bog (Cors Caron) in the west all have an abundance of peat-bog plants, insects and birds and are national nature reserves. Tregaron Bog is especially well-known as a good place to see red kites, the 'five-star' birds of Mid Wales. (Visitors here need a permit from the Nature Conservancy Council).

A home for plants

The unique combination of rocks and heights in the Brecon Beacons National Park gives it a special role as a habitat for plants and animals. Take the Old Red Sandstone, for instance, which rises to its highest levels in southern Britain below Brecon and Llandovery. Most sandstones break down into a limeless soil which – on high ground – can support only heather, bilberry and other lime-avoiders, but the local Old Red Sandstone is rich in lime. So wherever there are rock faces inaccessible to sheep, they may be clothed with lime-loving plants such as roseroot, mossy saxifrage, purple saxifrage, lesser meadow-rue (the mountain form), northern bedstraw, rock stonecrop and a little fern called green spleenwort. Some are true alpines, growing at the southern limit of their British range, and the best places to see these are at Tarren yr Esgob in the Black Mountains, the north face of the Beacons, Craig Cerrig-gleisiad, a national nature reserve six miles south-west of Brecon and, in the far west, the cliffs above Llyn y Fan Fach.

Rivers and their role

The streams which flow in all directions from the heartland of Mid Wales rise with alarming speed in heavy rain. As they rush by, brown with silt, it is easy to understand the huge part they have played in the shaping of the landscape. Today they support a wide range of water-based wildlife. The only fish to be found in some of the stony torrents is the brown trout, but others also have bullheads and stone loaches. The Severn, as it approaches the deep, fertile soils of Shropshire, is rich in a variety of fish: salmon, grayling, pike, perch, club, roach, dace, bleak, gudgeon, ruffe, eel and a fairly recent introduction, the barbel. The fertility of the River Wye increases markedly after it leaves the trout zone and approaches Builth having collected mineral-rich tributaries like the Ithon, the Irfon and the Chwefri. Below Builth the Wye flows over limy rocks, whose presence is indicated by the lime-loving wild chives which grow along the banks for several miles. By the time the river reaches the Old Red Sandstone near Hay it is brimming with coarse fish – huge numbers of chub, roach and dace. As in the Severn, there is an introduced population of barbel, and the Wye is also a famous salmon river.

After the Severn and Wye, perhaps the region's

The goosander, which is widespread in Scotland, only began breeding in Wales as recently as 1970; it can now be seen on the rivers Usk and Tywi

best-known rivers are the Usk and the Tywi, both much cherished by trout fishermen. Dippers, jolly-looking, rotund little birds which spend long periods standing on rocks bobbing up and down in a peculiar fashion, are often seen along these rivers, as are grey wagtails – elegant birds with lovely yellow underparts. Sandpipers nest along the rivers, but they are shy birds, most often seen flying low over the water, calling as they go. These days it is possible to see increasing numbers of goosander too, a fish-eating duck which first bred in Wales in 1970. In the far west the Teifi hastens down off the moorlands south of Plynlimon, slows up in the deep peat of Tregaron Bog and then flows away into West Wales, rich in many forms of aquatic life. The otter, now much declined in parts of Britain, still survives on this and many Mid Wales rivers.

In the extreme south of the Brecon Beacons National Park there are several delightful and unique streams. As they flow down the acid slopes of Fforest Fawr they are typical moorland torrents, but on reaching a band of limestone outcrop, they change abruptly. In this yielding rock the water has sliced out a region of deep gorges and waterfalls unlike any other in Wales. Naturalists have long been drawn to these shadowy ravines, rich in ferns, including brittle bladder-fern and green spleenwort. Meadow saxifrage, water avens, globe flowers and many others are also found here. The lime-rich water, teeming with invertebrates, attracts underwater feeders such as dippers. Pyrddin, Nedd, Mellte and Hepste are well-known rivers in this limestone country, easily reached from the Vale of Neath.

Lakes and reservoirs
Most of the lakes and reservoirs are up on the moorlands, many providing spectacular scenery –

as at Clywedog, Elan, Claerwen and Brianne. But their acidity greatly limits the number of plants, birds and other wildlife they can support. Better conditions are found on lower ground, where the reservoir near Talybont-on-Usk has up to a thousand ducks in winter and attracts passage waders, when the water levels are suitable. Four miles north, at Llangorse, is the largest natural lake in South Wales. This lowland water, partly choked by reeds and other plants, has long been known for its wealth of unusual plants and insects, for its breeding birds, winter wildfowl, passage waders and terns. Sadly, this fine lake has suffered much from disturbance and pollution for many years, but measures are now being taken to improve the situation. The Monmouthshire and Brecon Canal in the Usk Valley and Montgomeryshire Canal near Welshpool, are also of considerable botanical interest. The Monmouthshire and Brecon Canal is also one of the few places where kingfishers breed.

Welsh woodlands
Man has been clearing away the native woodland, which was mainly of oak, for so many centuries that only scattered remnants are now left, chiefly on steep hillsides. On acid soils the oak usually grows alongside birch and rowan, with heather, bilberry and grasses as ground cover. But on the more lime-rich soils, the oak is mixed with ash, wych elm, hazel, holly, hawthorn, sycamore and alder. On the Carboniferous Limestone there are ashwoods scattered with yews and whitebeams; and on the woodland floor lime-loving plants such as lily-of-the-valley and (in sunny clearings) common rockrose grow. Beech as a native tree just manages to get this far west; one of the best places to see it is in the gorge at Cwm Clydach, a national nature reserve near Abergavenny. Among other woodland national nature reserves are Coed Rheidol near Devil's Bridge; Allt Rhyd-y-groes near Llandovery; and Nant Irfon near Llanwrtyd-Wells.

Broad-leaved woodland is crucial to the survival of a vast number of plants and animals. The oak, especially, is a tree on which a multitude of insects feed, and they in turn are the food of many birds in spring and summer. Redstarts, wood warblers, willow warblers and pied flycatchers can all be found in these oakwoods, and there are also tits, woodpeckers, finches, thrushes, nuthatches and tree creepers. Most of the buzzards and kites seen circling over the moorlands come down to breed in the oakwoods, and this beautiful woodland is also a refuge for badger, stoat, weasel, polecat, hedgehog and a variety of mice, voles, shrews and bats. These days farmers and landowners are encouraged to rehabilitate neglected broad-leaved woodlands and even to plant new ones – a development that is certain to benefit wildlife.

Huge areas of conifers have been planted this century, mainly on the uplands. One effect of this is that the grassland and peat-bog birds – skylark, meadow pipit, buzzard, kite, raven, golden plover, dunlin, snipe and curlew – have lost large tracts of their natural habitat. On the other hand, whinchats, willow warblers, redpolls and black grouse have started to colonise the plantations, especially where the trees are young and bush-like. However, as the trees grow, they smother the vegetation beneath them, and then the only birds that can survive are those which inhabit the tree tops. These include goldcrests, siskins, crossbills and woodpigeons.

To the north-west, Mid Wales meets the sea at

Vast conifer plantations have attracted the goldcrest, whose nest hangs from the conifer branch

the beautiful Dyfi (Dovey) estuary – a superb locality for ducks, geese, waders and many other birds. The estuary is a national nature reserve, part of which is owned by the RSPB, who provide birdwatching facilities at Ynys-hir. The national nature reserve also includes Ynyslas sand dunes and the adjacent plant-rich peatland of Cors Fochno or Borth Bog. The peaty depths of this bog have revealed the perfectly preserved pollen from trees which grew in the area thousands of years ago.

There are many nature reserves scattered about the Mid Wales area. Details of their whereabouts and of the kind of wildlife they support can be obtained from the Nature Conservancy Council, RSPB and the county Wildlife Trusts. Their addresses are listed on pages 74 and 79, and a selection of reserves is provided on page 74.

Globe flowers thrive in the deep ravines carved out of limestone by the streams in the south of the Brecon Beacons National Park

The History of the Hills

The first impressions of the Brecon Beacons and Central Wales are of emptiness. This is a peaceful, thinly populated area of small market towns, country villages and isolated hamlets. Yet this part of Wales, for all its present peace and quiet, has witnessed the full flow of history.

The first inhabitants

These hills, valleys, mountains and borderlands tell a story which stretches from ancient stone monoliths to 19th-century lead mines. Man's first relationship with the landscape began in the mists of time. Palaeolithic (Old Stone Age) hunters in search of deer and ox probably roamed these hills and the forests which once clothed them 10,000 years BC. But we have to wait until Neolithic (New Stone Age) times for positive evidence of settlement in the Brecon Beacons.

Neolithic man, our first farmer, appeared around 5,000BC. He cut down primeval forests and introduced new farming techniques, initiating a profound revolution as he strove to master his environment. Neolithic communities must also have had impulses aspiring to the spiritual and religious (hardly compatible with our image of 'primitive' man), for they built ceremonial stone tombs in which to bury their dead. These tombs consisted of a stone framework which would originally have been covered by an earthen mound. In the Brecon Beacons, a number of fine examples survive, including the long cairn of Gwern-vale beside the A40 on the outskirts of Crickhowell, and the well-preserved rectangular chamber of Tŷ Elltud near the village of Llanhamlach a few miles from Brecon.

Neolithic times gradually gave way to a culture based on more efficient metal tools and implements. The Bronze Age, a few thousand years

BC, saw the replacement of the earlier communal graves with individual burial mounds of stone or earth. These are scattered liberally across high ground throughout South and Central Wales. Many a hill has its Bronze Age cairns. Amateur archaeologists, armed with suitably detailed maps, can quite easily seek out such sites for themselves – in the wild, remote uplands south-east of Tregaron, for example, or on the hills around Rhayader, or at the summit of Corn Du, a 2,863ft neighbour of Pen y Fan in the central Beacons.

Strange monuments

It was also around this time that the most striking and mysterious monuments in the Brecon Beacons appeared. Drive across the moors of Fforest Fawr north of the village of Ystradfellte and, just before the road plunges down a hairpinned escarpment, you will see a solitary standing stone, all alone and miles from anywhere at the head of the valley. This is Maen Llia, one of around 30 such stones in the Beacons park.

Of similar antiquity (around 2000-1300BC) are the Brecon Beacons stone circles, the best of which is Cerrig Duon, a ring of 20 stones a few miles along the mountain road north of the A4067 near Craig-y-nos. Intriguingly, they may well have some kind of relationship to a second group of stones, Saith Maen, which stand a few miles away and are aligned in such a way as to point to Cerrig Duon.

These strange sites induce speculation, but no mystery surrounds Wales's Iron Age hill forts. These were built from around 600BC as strongholds for Iron Age communities and their livestock, and as focal points of tribal power. Fine examples crown many a hill or prominent position. There is, for instance, a remarkable concentration of hill forts in north Dyfed between Aberystwyth and Tal-y-bont. The Black Mountain region of the Brecon Beacons National Park contains possibly the most impressive stronghold of all. Here, on a bracken-clad ridge above the fertile Vale of Tywi, stands one of the largest hill forts in Wales. Covering around 30 acres, Garn Goch still retains its earthen defences and stone ramparts, which in part survive remarkably intact. Greater imagination may be needed at some of the Beacons' other 20 or so weatherbeaten hill forts, though the examples at Pen-y-crug (near Brecon), Castell Dinas (near

Prehistoric life has left its trace on the Mid Wales landscape. Garn Goch hill fort can be seen south of Llangadog; and Maen Llia (inset) is one of many ancient standing stones

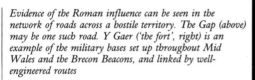

Evidence of the Roman influence can be seen in the network of roads across a hostile territory. The Gap (above) may be one such road. Y Gaer ('the fort', right) is an example of the military bases set up throughout Mid Wales and the Brecon Beacons, and linked by well-engineered routes

Talgarth) and Crug Hywel (on Table Mountain above Crickhowell) display well-preserved earthworks – and, incidentally, quite stunning views.

The Roman conquest

The famous Roman boast, *Veni, Vidi, Vici* ('I came, I saw, I conquered') became increasingly tentative, the deeper they ventured into highland Wales. They arrived in Britain in force in AD43, and soon overran most of the south. Wales proved a more difficult nut to crack. It took them until about AD80 to complete their conquest of Wales by establishing a network of fortified camps and military roads. But only in the extreme south-east of Wales were they able to introduce the kind of civilian settlements common in their conquered territories in lowland Britain. The stubborn native tribes of the Brecon Beacons and Central Wales probably proved more resistant to Roman influences.

The Romans' achievements were nonetheless impressive. All roads around what is now Llandrindod Wells would have led to Castell Collen, a Roman stronghold securely sited on the banks of the River Ithon. In the Beacons, the best-preserved Roman site can be found at Y Gaer ('the fort') in farmlands just west of Brecon, where the remains of a key base capable of accommodating 500 cavalry have been excavated.

The Romans' most memorable legacy, especially within the National Park, is their road system. From Y Gaer, a route runs due west, past Y Pigwn camp on the moors above Trecastle, to Llandovery. More contentiously, a southern route from Brecon is thought to have been forged straight through the central Beacons massif. This,

the well-known 'Gap' trackway, crests a 1,961ft break in the ridge below Pen y Fan and, if Roman in origin, would have connected Y Gaer with a Roman base at Merthyr Tydfil. Other routes probably led northwards (to Castell Collen) and south-eastwards (to the main legionary base at Caerleon). But the most satisfying stretch of trackway is the Sarn Helen route which strikes out south-west of Y Gaer across Fforest Fawr to the Roman forts at Coelbren and Neath. The remoteness of the terrain has left this well-engineered track intact for some miles. Walkers can pick it up where it joins the mountain road a few miles north of Ystradfellte, and follow it across gloriously empty countryside. Along the way, look out for the standing stone known as Maen Madoc. This slender 9ft pillar stone is a rare example of the way in which Roman and native Celtic cultures must inevitably have intermingled during the hundreds of years of occupation.

The most unusual Roman site in Wales is hidden away deep in the hills at Pumsaint, south-east of Lampeter. Pumsaint's Dolaucothi mines are the only place in Britain where it has been established definitely that the Romans dug for gold. Their adits and incredibly sophisticated aqueduct systems can still be traced among silent, wooded slopes where thousands of slaves once mined the precious metal for the Imperial Mint at Lyons.

New invaders

The Romans left around AD400, their empire in ruins. The vacuum was filled, unfortunately for the native Welsh, by new invaders. Saxons, Picts and Irish Goidel tribes brought with them a Dark Age. The only positive glimmers came in the 6th century, when pioneering monk-missionaries began

Medieval designs adorn the tiles in Strata Florida Abbey (top), a Cistercian house founded in 1164, which became the political, religious and educational centre of the country in the 12th and 13th centuries. Also dating from the 12th century, White Castle (above) stands on the site of an early Norman fortification

to travel the land preaching the early Christian message.

The unassuming little village of Llanddewi-Brefi near Tregaron is clustered around a church which is traditionally the site of a famous gathering in AD 519, attended by St David, Wales's patron saint. Here, fact and fiction possibly collide, for the ground is said to have risen beneath David's feet so that he could be heard by the crowds, a legend probably not unconnected with the fact that the meeting was held on the site now occupied by the 12th-century parish church, which stands on a rise above the village's rooftops.

Further north, just inland from Aberystwyth, the grand church at Llanbadarn Fawr looks too large for its village setting. All is explained by its history, for the imposing church, dating from about 1200, was built on a religious site of great significance, founded by St Padarn in the 6th century.

Monuments to early religious faith can be found in many a church setting. At Llanddewi in the hills above Brecon, the neat little cruciform Church of St David was first mentioned as a religious site in AD500. Nearby Llangorse grew up around a church which can be traced back to a community of monks founded by St Paulinus, tutor to St David. Mynydd Illtud, the grassy common south-east of Brecon, is named after St Illtud, Wales's most influential early Christian leader along with St David. According to legend, Illtud is buried on the common beneath a mound of stones at Bedd Illtud.

Monasticism was to leave a deep impression in these parts. Most influential of all were the Cistercians, a white-robed order who brought with them far more than a spiritual message. These dynamic medieval monks were industrious improvers of their environment, and are credited with the successful introduction of sheep farming to the hills of South and Central Wales, as well as the building of roads and bridges. Their greatest shrine is Strata Florida Abbey, in the foothills north-east of Tregaron, a tranquil ruin which was once 'the Westminster Abbey of Wales'.

The Norman forces

The bellicose side of the medieval period is represented by the sombre stone castles which survive here. The Norman Conquest was in some ways similar to the Roman invasion of 1,000 years earlier. Norman influences were at their strongest in the valleys and lowlands. A concentration of castles in the border country of south-east Wales reflects the dominant hold which the Marcher lords had over their Welsh territories: the so-called 'Three Castles', for example, of Grosmont, Skenfrith and White (at Llantilio Crossenny), which formed a defensive triangle in the rolling borderlands east of Abergavenny.

The impression remains of a Norman sphere of influence, centred around castles, fortified towns and a feudal system of farming, which had a diluted impact in the native upland communities. In the mountains of the central and eastern Beacons, for example, life probably went on much as before, even though Brecon itself became an important seat of Norman power, protected by a castle and ring of town walls. Further east, the story was different. Here, in the more manageable, more arable lowlands, the Normans were able to impose their feudal farming practices overseen by the lord of the manor.

Today's landscapes still reflect this partial Anglo-Norman dominance. Settled farming patterns and villages of manorial origin characterise the gentler, fertile east of this region, while unenclosed common pastures and mountains fill the rugged west. Place names say it all. Compare, for example, borderland Walton, straight out of the Home Counties, with Pontrhydfendigaid, just over 30 miles to the west. Language is also revealing. Around Crickhowell in the east of the National Park, Welsh is spoken by probably less than five per cent of the population, a figure which rises gradually to around 70 per cent in the far west of the park.

One site above all others marks the transition from troubled medieval times to the more settled later Middle Ages. Tretower Court and Castle is a unique place at which a sturdy round tower, put up in the 12th century, stands next to a handsome stone and timber dwelling built a few hundred years later, when considerations of comfort were beginning to replace those of conflict.

Industrial legacy

The green landscapes of the Beacons and Mid Wales's hill country to the north give an impression of timelessness, of remaining unusually faithful to their rural roots. Yet these hills have known the hand of industry. Mid Wales has a history of silver and lead mining dating back to Roman times, an activity that reached its peak in the 18th and 19th centuries. Much of Britain's silver and lead ore once came from Cwmystwyth, a remote spot between Aberystwyth and Rhayader. Driving across the narrow Cwmystwyth mountain road, travellers suddenly come across a wholly unexpected sight: the rusting remains of a large mine, standing in a strange, lunar-like landscape of spoil heaps and detritus.

Occasional gouges in the hillsides and strangely shaped grassy humps and bumps, now grazed by sheep, are all that are left of the smaller mines,

though at Bryn Tail (on the shores of Llyn Clywedog) and Llywernog (near Ponterwyd), there are old sites that have been specially preserved for visitors.

Matching – and surpassing – the mining activity on the northern rim of the region was the frenetic industrial exploitation that occurred along the southern boundary of the Brecon Beacons. The explosive growth of the coal and iron industries was almost entirely confined to the South Wales valleys, though there were incursions into the fringes of the Beacons (at Clydach, for example, and in the hills north of Merthyr Tydfil) to quarry limestone for the local ironworks. The only serious monument to industrial activity with the National Park itself is now, appropriately enough, the epitome of scenic tranquillity. There is no better way to enjoy the pastoral Vale of Usk than to cruise the waters, or walk along the towpath, of the Monmouthshire and Brecon Canal, originally built to serve the nearby mines and quarries.

Tretower Castle (right) was built by the Normans to guard against the unconquered Welsh; Tretower Court (below), once the mansion of the Vaughans, is an unusually complete medieval manor house

Traces of Industry

This is a land normally associated with thinly populated, open moors where buzzards and red kite maintain their lonely vigil. Yet a little exploration and investigation will soon reveal some of its industrial archaeological secrets, among the thickly wooded valleys and open hills.

Upland treasures
It was treasure richer than the mines of Peru that drew industry into the remote uplands, where the highly faulted sedimentary shales and grits were interwoven with deposits of lead, silver and gold. Metal mining can be traced to the Roman occupation of Wales, gradually increasing during the Middle Ages and accelerating rapidly during the 18th and 19th centuries. Other industries encroached upon the countryside, too: the growing need for constant supplies of water for Birmingham Corporation saw the transformation of the Elan Valley in the early years of this century; and further south the Brecon Beacons rub shoulders with the huge Welsh coalfield.

Farming is the main industry of the area, although that, too, has undergone many changes; but milking, haymaking and shearing are still part of the well established order of life. The land is dotted with reminders of the days of transhumance in the names of the homesteads – 'hafod', the temporary upland summer dwelling, and 'hendre', the permanent home in the lower lying land.

Forest riches
The most visible change on the landscape has been the steady increase in the softwood plantations which have, to a great measure, replaced the native

Timber-felling was a particularly tough job when native hardwoods covered the Welsh mountains

hardwoods. At felling times the forests are now assailed by the buzzing chainsaw instead of handaxes and crosscut saws. Although not great in number, sawing mills were widespread and more often than not powered by water. Even during the halcyon days of steam, the remoteness of the industrial locations dictated the continued use of water power and waterwheels and Pelton wheels were at work on the farms and especially in the many metal mines.

The metal heritage
The valuable ores are usually found in thin deposits following the fault lines in the shales. Occasionally it is possible to see where the early miners located such deposits and followed them across the land by opening ditches, called 'rakes'. Examples of this method can be traced at Rhandirmwyn, near

The scenic Vale of Rheidol Railway was once used by the lead mines, whose waste scarred the landscape

The changing face of industry: at the Roman gold mines at Pumsaint, near Lampeter, the original workings can still be traced (top). The mines were reopened in 1888–1910 and again in 1933–38 (centre and above), but neither occasion brought lasting returns, and the mining did not affect the Roman workings

Industrial evidence

Most of the mine remains date from the 19th century although metal has been mined in the region for over 1,000 years. The formation of the Society of Mines Royal during the reign of Elizabeth I saw an increase in mining activity to the south-east of Aberystwyth. In the 18th century a group of entrepreneurs, the Company of Mine Adventurers, broke the monopoly of the Mines Royal and thus heralded a period of freewheeling enterprise.

With the technological advancement of the 19th century more mines were opened, until the industry reached its zenith by the 1880s. The most widespread of minerals was lead, sometimes intermingled with worthwhile deposits of silver – sufficient quantities were available to warrant the establishment of a Mint at Aberystwyth in the 17th century.

One of the most productive mines was located around the remote village of Rhandirmwyn. Mining began there in earnest in the early years of the 18th century and continued until 1932. Without doubt, this was one of the most successful mines; the account books for the period 1775 to 1797 show a profit of £86,707 13s 1½d.

Most of the lead mines had to rely upon horse-drawn transport, although those around Devil's Bridge were able to take advantage of the Vale of Rheidol Railway that was opened in 1902 to link with the main line at Aberystwyth. Ironically, its opening coincided with a sharp decline in mining and its survival is a quite remarkable story of official oversight and near closure. Luckily, the narrow gauge steam locomotives and carriages still negotiate the winding scenic route, climbing 600ft

Llandovery, where they were the precursors of a large lead mining complex using boats to carry the ore from underground.

Whenever possible the metal mines were de-watered by adits driven at the lowest levels to drain the workings, and at many of the lead mining sites the location of the veins can be traced on the hillsides from the adit entrances.

If water underground was the miner's bane it was a positive boon on the surface, as it provided a much needed energy source to drive many waterwheels used for pumping, winding and powering the separating and dressing machinery. Steam power was used mainly to work the large pumping engines and at a few sites there are remains of the 'Cornish' style engine houses. Mid Wales attracted metal miners from a wide area; in the early 1900s some 200 Italians were employed at the Frongoch mine near Pontrhydygroes. The combination of Welsh and Italian with a sprinkling of Cornish for good measure produced a volatile concoction that, on a number of occasions, resulted in rather boisterous confrontations.

Cwmystwyth's lead waste robbed much of the surrounding valley of its vegetation, but the ruined buildings are now a dramatic feature of the countryside. The Llywernog Silver-Lead mines near Ponterwyd (above) reached their peak of activity in the 1880s, though prospecting started in the 1740s. Restoration began in 1973, and the buildings now form part of the Lead and Silver Mining Museum. At Nant-yr-Arian, a 2-mile Forestry Commission walk follows moorland and woodland – where miners once toiled (below)

above sea level to the three superimposed arches at Devil's Bridge.

The history of metal mining in the area is well documented at the Llywernog Lead and Silver Mining Museum, near Ponterwyd, alongside the A44 road between Llangurig and Aberystwyth where the actual mine buildings form part of the museum displays, and a number of waterwheels are at work.

The landscapes of metal mining can be quite extraordinary, and none more so than at Cwmystwyth. Large areas of the valley are devoid of vegetation because of the high toxic content of the waste tips, and scattered everywhere are chunks of quartz and galena. The valley floor is littered with ruined buildings, the largest being the former crushing house with its corrugated sheeting hanging loosely to bang and creak in the wind – a melancholy remnant of a long history of human endeavour. Traces of early mining techniques are visible near the tiny village of Pumsaint near Lampeter, where deposits of gold attracted the legions of Imperial Rome around AD75.

King coal
Between 1740 and 1850 a 'great chain of iron furnaces' and their towns appeared along the northern edge of the South Wales coalfield adjoining the boundary of the National Park where massive deposits of limestone, coal and ironstone were present. The coal measures outcrop along a band about 40 miles long and vary from hard anthracite through to good quality bituminous and steam coal. In places it was possible to mine ironstone and coal together, and substantial deposits of limestone underlying the coal measures outcropped just a short distance to the north. So while furnaces bubbled and coal tips grew in the valleys to the south, industrialisation made its mark on the upland areas.

There are many places where the old ironstone levels enter into the hillsides but far more apparent are the areas of 'patches', where the topsoil was removed to reveal the veins of iron and the seams of coal. Hundreds of acres of land were turned over and although derelict land reclamation has swept much away there are still areas to the north of the Heads of the Valleys Road (A465) where the old working faces and their 'finger' tips spread across the land.

The Clydach Gorge between Abergavenny and Brynmawr is an industrial archaeologists' paradise; within its confines (3½ miles long by ½ mile wide) are crammed the remains of charcoal and coke burning iron furnaces, lime kilns and quarries, tramroads, the trackbed of the Merthyr Tydfil and Abergavenny Railway clinging to the side of the gorge, a cast iron bridge dated 1824, industrial housing and, just to complete the story, the Monmouthshire and Brecon Canal, touching the eastern end of the valley.

Water has played a vital role in the industrial life of Wales. An early version of the commuter train carried workers to the Ystradfellte Waterworks (top) and the 'Mon and Brec Canal' (above) was used for commercial traffic until 1932

Canal trail

The length of canal from Brecon to Pontypool, where it links with the Monmouthshire Canal, was completed in 1812. It is navigable along its whole length within the National Park and time spent walking its towpath or moving gently along by boat leads to many fascinating sites. One of the most delightful is the complex at Llanfoist where an incline that served Hills tramroad (1818) terminates at a warehouse and loading wharf. The trackbed of the tramroad is easily followed as it climbs sharply up the Blorenge mountain before levelling out to pass underneath the site of an iron forge, opened in 1816. Clinging tenaciously to the hillside it then sweeps around the head of the valley into limestone quarries, before passing through a 1½-mile long tunnel (now blocked) to Blaenafon, where the remains of the ironworks and the Big Pit Mining Museum are popular visitor attractions.

The abandoned tramroads often pass through quite magnificent scenery. High above Abercraf (Abercrave) at the head of the Swansea Valley John Christie's tramroad, opened in 1825, follows a winding route from the Swansea Canal deep into the rural heartland of the Brecon Beacons. Its construction made economic sense by providing a

Coalmining started in earnest in Blaenafon in 1782, as coal replaced wood in fuelling ironworks

means of communication into the farming areas so that food could be carried into the intensely industrialised Swansea Valley. In 1867 the Neath and Brecon Railway was opened to passenger traffic following the route planned and engineered by the tramroad builders.

At Penwyllt is a small station that has close links with the world of opera. The great 19th-century diva Madame Adelina Patti owned Craig-y-nos, a large house in the valley (see page 44), and such was her status that rooms in the station were suitably furnished and set aside for her use. It is reported that whenever she left to undertake a grand tour the Station Masters en route down the Swansea Valley sported their best uniforms and the town bands played her through every station; proof perhaps that Wales is, indeed, a musical nation.

As well as the great opera star the railway carried goods traffic, including the much sought-after silica bricks manufactured at Penwyllt, where there are still remains of the beehive kilns. Silica bricks were used to line furnaces, and such was their quality that they reached worldwide markets; orders were even received from Russia.

Lime legacy

Limestone was worked across the southern slopes of the Brecon Beacons, and even the so-called 'rotten stone', a decomposed limestone, was quarried and used as an abrasive and cleaning agent in tinplate works. Numbers of kilns in varying states of repair are to be found in most areas, and those on the top of the Black Mountain, close to the A4069 between Brynamman and Llangadog, provide a sensational viewing place looking northwards over Dyffryn Tywi. Because quicklime was so important to 'sweeten' the acid soils of the uplands, groups of farmers occasionally formed combinations to finance quarrying and kiln construction. Perhaps the most flamboyant kilns are those at Llandybïe near Ammanford. Dating from 1858 they were designed by the architect Richard Kyrke Penson and his drawings were exhibited at the Royal Academy in that year. When viewed from inside the loading bays the pointed Gothic arches are church-like, and the exterior is enhanced with pointed blanked arcading and a corbelled cornice.

Down the line

To the south of the region the coalfield-dictated railway construction reached outwards from the valleys to link with the midlands of England and North Wales. The Brecon and Merthyr Railway Company opened a way across the Brecon Beacons in 1863, and in doing so created the highest railway tunnel (1,300ft above sea level) in Britain. Part of the former trackbed north of Merthyr Tydfil has been re-laid with narrow gauge metals and carries the Brecon Mountain Railway that presently terminates alongside the Taf Fechan Reservoir.

Crossing diagonally from Swansea to Shrewsbury, the Central Wales Railway was opened in 1868 to provide the means of getting the high quality Welsh coals and the iron, steel and tinplate products to wider markets. Besides that, it also gave access to the spa towns, the largest of which, Llandrindod Wells, attracted over 80,000 visitors each season in its peak years. Trains waited at the station for up to 15 minutes while the passengers and their luggage were off-loaded. Mercifully the station has not suffered much from 'improvements' and retains its original charm, as does the whole of the line; an opportunity to travel its length should not be missed.

A rail trip to Aberystwyth is also a special event, if only to visit a monument to railway failure and educational success. After the Cambrian Railway was opened for passenger traffic in 1864 Thomas Savin, one of its promoters, invested a small fortune in the construction of a large, luxury hotel which was to put Aberystwyth on the package tour map. Alas, his dreams foundered in bankruptcy before the building was completed, but it was a heaven-sent opportunity for Welsh educationalists, who purchased and completed the building to house the University of Wales. Among the tourist attractions is the funicular Cliff Railway that was opened in 1896 and gave access to a camera obscura, recently reconstructed. Before the railways it was, of course, the sea that served the transport needs of the town and the harbour was completed in 1834 when the hinterland began to produce lead and silver in large quantities. Lime kilns and a small brewery were built along the quayside, and the harbour provided a safe refuge for the small fishing fleet.

The Big Pit at Blaenafon, showing the 18th-century underground engine pit level

Taking the Waters

While the spas in other parts of Britain are some distance apart – and our ancestors would have had to 'change the horses' several times to travel between them – those in Mid Wales are all within an area of 20 miles or so. They were used well before the Victorian heyday, at a time when they could only be reached by coaches bumping over muddy tracks. It says a lot for the stamina of the visitors who, if they had not been in need of 'the cure' when they started their journey, must certainly have qualified for treatment by the time they arrived!

Fresh discoveries
There are interesting accounts of how the various waters were discovered – or perhaps re-discovered would be more correct, for the Romans occupied this area, and whoever heard of any self respecting Roman leaving a spring undiscovered and unused?

Llanwrtyd-Wells, the southern-most spa in the chain, has a spring with the highest sulphur content in the country and in 1732 the Reverend Theophilus Evans, led by recommendation and following his nose, hesitated even to try it until the sight of a frog very much alive in the spring convinced him that the water wasn't as poisonous as it smelt. This proved to be a wise conclusion because after using it regularly – for drinking and washing – he was completely cured of a very serious skin disease which had been troubling him for some time. Anyone walking the banks of the River Irfon these days will appreciate his hesitation, for the well which was built later is still there, and if you are down wind, it is easy to understand why the spot was once called Ffynnon Drewllyd (Stinking Spring). It was later re-named Dol y coed. More springs were discovered in 1897 by which time Llanwrtyd could offer magnesium, saline and chalybeate water at the Victoria Wells.

The old town of Builth Wells also offered saline, chalybeate and sulphur water. The latter is mentioned as early as 1740, but the saline spring does not appear to have been discovered until 1830, when a party of mowers stumbled across it, and the stream which ran from the spring became known as Nant yr Halen (Salt Brook). Builth soon had two popular centres – Park Wells and Glannau.

A spring containing rare barium chloride – a much sought after remedy for heart conditions – was found in Llangammarch Wells by a cotter out searching for a lost pig. Records say he found it to have a 'vile taste.' Although the village also possessed sulphur springs, it was for the barium water that it became famous. Even now, there are still enquiries about it.

Forgotten springs
Little or no mention is made these days of the once well-known Llandegley spa, which was situated a few miles north-east of Llandrindod Wells. Sulphur and chalybeate springs were recorded in 1825 but although the village still exists, there is nothing left of this once popular watering place but an old wooden hut and a rather unsavoury ditch.

The saline spring in Llandrindod Wells was in use in the late 17th century by the Vaughan family. A Mrs Jenkins came across sulphur water near the same site in 1736, and her 'cures' became well known locally. About a century later the Pump House Hotel was built near the spot.

In the valley, another spring eventually came to light. A Mr Pilot was said to have dreamed of its existence and location and, on waking and going to investigate, found his dream was true. At least one member of this gentleman's family was traced not so long ago, living in nearby Newtown. In fact, Mr Pilot had been erecting a tent in which his employers were to hold an auction when he found the spring.

Healing properties?
The wide variety of spa waters in Mid Wales was valued as a treatment for a whole host of conditions. Chalybeate water was taken for anaemia and general debility; while sulphur water seems to have been

considered good for almost anything, from skin complaints to kidney and bladder diseases. A combination of sulphur and saline treatment was recommended for sufferers of gout and rheumatism. Magnesium must have been good for digestive ailments, and it was also prescribed for tubercular-related illnesses. But prescription was a key word. To quote an 1897 Guide Book, 'better stay at home than subject one's organisation to the careless use of these waters.'

Attracting the crowds

With one exception, there is nothing to suggest that much more than fairly local use was made of the various springs in Mid Wales until about a hundred years had passed. That exception was the area which eventually became Llandrindod Wells. In 1748 some verses praising the water there were published in the *Gentlemen's Magazine*, causing an upsurge of interest. Encouraged by this, a Mr Grosvenor built what can only be described as a hotel complex, providing for every possible need – a necessary service, in such a remote place. The

Llandrindod Wells gained fame and fortune from its saline and sulphur water, dispensed from the municipal Pump Room at Rock Park, and from the railway, which brought in the crowds from 1867

hotel was very well patronised, although there seem to have been a lot of complaints from the local inhabitants about the morals of the occupants, who were branded as 'fashionable gamesters and libertines'. After it closed some time after 1787, there was a decline and although an erudite work by a Dr Wessel Linden in 1756 placed great importance upon the properties of the medicinal waters, Llandrindod, like the other spas in the area, had to wait until the mid-19th century to reach the height of its popularity.

Around 1865, the railway line was built linking up the spas with South Wales, and with its arrival came an influx of visitors, resulting in property development on a scale completely out of proportion to the local population. The largest of the spas was Llandrindod Wells, home to only 180

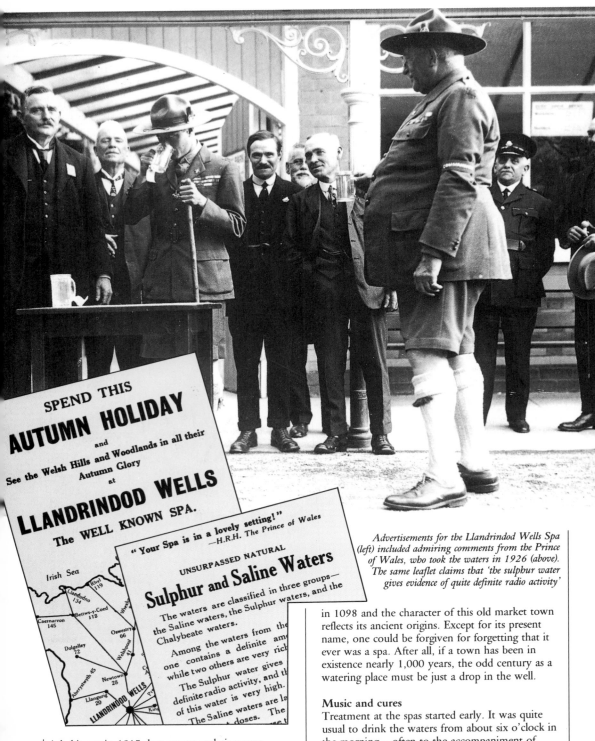

SPEND THIS
AUTUMN HOLIDAY
and
See the Welsh Hills and Woodlands in all their
Autumn Glory
at
LLANDRINDOD WELLS
The WELL KNOWN SPA.

"Your Spa is in a lovely setting!"
—H.R.H. The Prince of Wales

UNSURPASSED NATURAL
Sulphur and Saline Waters

The waters are classified in three groups—
the Saline waters, the Sulphur waters, and the
Chalybeate waters.

Among the waters from the
one contains a definite amo
while two others are very rich

The Sulphur water gives
definite radio activity, and th
of this water is very high.
The Saline waters are la
doses. The

Advertisements for the Llandrindod Wells Spa (left) included admiring comments from the Prince of Wales, who took the waters in 1926 (above). The same leaflet claims that 'the sulphur water gives evidence of quite definite radio activity'

inhabitants in 1817, but accommodating over 80,000 visitors by the 1890s. Today the great Victorian terraces give evidence of the sudden, massive property demand: custom built for the requirements of the gentlefolk, many have five floors. From the hills around Llandrindod, the sight of these large buildings amidst open country is rather a shock!

Llanwrtyd-Wells, on the other hand, sits close up against its magnificent mountains and only some four miles away, little Llangammarch seems to have been even more discreet in its development.

With the exception of the now unsung Llandegley, Builth Wells is the only one of these watering places whose appearance does not, today, seem to shout 'spa'. Builth was already a township

in 1098 and the character of this old market town reflects its ancient origins. Except for its present name, one could be forgiven for forgetting that it ever was a spa. After all, if a town has been in existence nearly 1,000 years, the odd century as a watering place must be just a drop in the well.

Music and cures
Treatment at the spas started early. It was quite usual to drink the waters from about six o'clock in the morning – often to the accompaniment of music. The day would be punctuated by entertainment, exercise and visits to the spa; queues two miles long were not unknown. It seems strange that anyone would wish to wait so long to drink such unpalatable liquid in large quantities, or to indulge in 'cures' such as the 'passing of electrodes through the system' and bathing in radio-active mud.

Over 30 treatments were available in all, the simplest being a glass of the waters. This came at an average cost of one penny, but it could be bought with a day ticket and as it was thought necessary to drink six or eight pints in some cases, this was probably the most economical way of going about it.

The atmosphere of Llandrindod Wells in its Victorian heyday is recreated every September, when everyone in the town dons the costume of the period for a week-long Victorian festival

Strict rules were laid down about 'taking the waters'. Readers of books of the period would find reminders that the sulphur water was a purgative of no mean order and 'should on no account be taken in the afternoon'. The same book goes on to explain that 'when thrown on hot iron it emits a blue flame and smells like brimstone – silver leaves have been changed in less than six minutes to a fine gold colour.' It then advises that the water is best adapted as an artificial bath.

The cure often involved a strenuous regime. Medical advisers suggested that saline water was at its best between March and November and should be drunk at about six or seven o'clock in the morning. Bleeding was generally recommended beforehand, and nothing was to be taken between meals other than the waters and plenty of exercise.

Upstairs and downstairs

Taking the waters was not the prerogative of the gentry; the spas catered for all classes. Many people from industrial South Wales came to sample the cure, and Llanwrtyd-Wells was a popular venue for travellers from Merthyr Tydfil and Swansea. There seems to have been a preponderance of upper class visitors to Llandrindod Wells. The Pump House Hotel even had two tariffs – for first and second class visitors. Many arrived to rent apartments, bringing their own servants to cater for them. The whole place, being a 'new town' was geared to its guests, and pavilions, halls, a 14-acre lake and a large church were all built to accommodate their needs. Llandrindod had its share of celebrities, too: Lloyd George was a frequent visitor, and the Prince of Wales – later to become the Duke of Windsor – took the waters here. One important guest in Llangammarch Wells was more discreet. In 1912, an entry was recorded as 'Prince and Princess of Munster from Germany'. This was apparently the Kaiser and his family – no doubt attracted by the famous barium water. Rich and

poor alike flocked in their thousands to Mid Wales, for the spas had become famous and fashionable and the cures had proved to be effective.

Today, Llandrindod Wells is the only one in Wales to survive as a working spa. The waters are still drunk by the glass in the Pump Room but fortunately one is no longer invited to sit in radioactive mud! The spa's heyday is re-enacted at the end of every summer, when the Llandrindod Victorian Festival turns back the clock for nine days. Victorian shop windows, inhabitants and visitors in 19th-century garb; horse buses, carriages and authentic entertainment help everyone to experience what it was like in the days when the spas of Mid Wales were the region's main attraction. This popular event may herald a revival of the faith in good air and natural remedies. There is a growing interest in British spas – people on the continent cannot understand why they ever declined – and along this little thread of Welsh watering places, many springs are still there, waiting to be rediscovered.

Sheep Farming

Sheep have always been the mainstay of the economic life of Mid Wales, and it is no coincidence that a number of sheep breeds found in all parts of the United Kingdom have their origins in the county of Powys. The region's importance as a centre of the wool, textile and leather industries has largely been due to the vast flocks of sheep grazing on the hills of Mid Wales.

Of course the sheep is something far more than a producer of wool: it is a source of meat, milk and manure as well as a supplier of skins and wool. Until the late 1940s one could still buy small quantities of the richly-flavoured, sheep-milk cheese in Brecon market; while in earlier times, cheese was regarded as a prize delicacy in many rural areas of Mid Wales. Sheep also played a crucial role in the maintenance of soil fertility, especially in the Middle Ages. By day sheep grazed on the common pasture land, but at night they were penned on the arable land to provide the manure that they trod into the soil to fertilize it. Mutton and lamb often provided the basis for *cawl*, that unique broth of meat and vegetables which was the mainstay of the diet of the rural Welsh.

The drovers

Mid Wales is by tradition a pastoral country and animals and animal products were almost its sole export until the 18th century. So important was livestock farming to the economy of the region that vast herds of black cattle and flocks of sheep were driven on the hoof to the markets of London and the Home Counties. These animals were driven across country, by-passing roads wherever possible so as not to pay tolls – and also to protect the animals' hooves. Here and there on the hills of Mynydd Eppynt and the Brecon Beacons were the hostelries and enclosures where the drovers and their animals stopped overnight before continuing on their daytime trek to the east.

The drovers themselves were a hardy and romantic body of men who carried a great deal of responsibility. In addition to maintaining the animal trade, they conducted business for their fellow countrymen in London – conveying rents to absentee landlords in the metropolis, paying local taxes to the Exchequer, and bringing back all manner of fashionable goods from London to their native districts. The drovers were also unofficial bankers for the people, and many actually founded banks in such market towns as Brecon, Llandovery Tregaron and Aberystwyth.

Sheep breeds

Throughout Mid Wales there are hardy breeds of sheep, capable of living in a mountain environment that is often very harsh. Their presence in such numbers has had the effect of transforming what would otherwise be a barren wasteland into a reservoir of store animals. Most of the animal breeds traditionally found on the farms of Powys are mountain types, but these have also adapted to the particular environment in which they flourish.

Welsh Mountain: Tan-faced, small sheep that resulted from the inter-breeding of the white-faced sheep imported by Roman invaders and the native, wild Soay sheep. The Welsh Mountain are the smallest of the British sheep breeds, and they have existed in the mountainous core of Wales for nearly two thousand years. The cold, wet conditions in the uplands of Powys are not really conducive to fine fleeces, but nevertheless the woollen industry in the remote valleys of Mid Wales was once largely dependent on the wool of mountain sheep, producing cloth which was rough and uneven in texture.

Black Welsh Mountain: This is now a recognised breed created by selecting black lambs from flocks of Mountain sheep. The fleece of the black sheep was once considered undesirable because of its inability to accept dyes, and at one time black sheep were regarded as mere decorative flocks for parklands. In recent years, though, the natural

Sheep come in all shapes and sizes in Mid Wales, and can be seen in the lowlands and the harsh mountain environment. From the top, right: Black Welsh Mountain sheep; Beulah Speckle Face; Brecknock Hill Cheviots; a Hill Radnor sheep; and a Clun ewe with her lambs. The main picture shows sheep grazing in Radnor Forest

black-brown fleeces with a soft texture have been in considerable demand for hand-loom weavers.

Badger-faced sheep (Defaid Torddu): An animal with a white face, which has the very distinctive marking of two black stripes running down the face and a black band down the chest and under the body. This breed was officially recognised in 1977, and Mid Wales can now lay claim to a number of flocks.

Beulah Speckle Face: These sheep occur widely on the Eppynt hills around the village of Beulah in south-west Powys – so much so that they were once known as the Eppynt Hill breed. The ewes are regarded as excellent breeders, providing high quality lambs, and the wool is used to produce high quality fabrics, with the coarser wool used in carpet manufacturing.

Brecknock Hill Cheviot: Scottish settlers, attracted to Mid Wales during the enclosures of the Great Forest of Brecknock, introduced this breed in the 1820s. The Cheviot thrives on the Old Red Sandstone soils on the northern slopes of the Brecon Beacons and barely survives when moved to other areas, even those a few miles away from the sandstone.

The wool of the Brecknock Cheviot, known locally as the Sennybridge Cheviot, is white, dense and uniform in quality and widely used to make fine tweeds.

Sheep-dipping was quite a picturesque affair when this photograph was taken at Glamsk Home Farm, Powys

Hill Radnor: Although these sheep are closely related to the Welsh Mountain, the kinder climatic conditions of their native Radnor has produced a less hardy but larger and more docile animal, producing what has been described as the best wool in Wales. During the 18th century it was in great demand from the woollen manufacturers of Powys for fine flannels and tweeds with a slightly rough finish.

Kerry Hill: This is a considerably larger animal than the mountain sheep and occurs widely in the hills around the village of Kerry, near Newtown, in central Powys. With a black muzzle and very white wool, the Kerry Hill is a very distinctive breed of sheep. Its wool, which is capable of taking dye of delicate pastel shades, was widely used to make fine flannels, the main produce of the old Montgomeryshire woollen industry.

Clun Forest: A very popular sheep found in many parts of Britain but originating in the gentle hills around the border village of Clun. These sheep are very adaptable to soil and climatic conditions and the ewes are considered excellent for breeding. Clun Forest sheep are reputed by many to produce the finest wool in Britain, widely used in the hosiery and knitting industries.

Many other breeds which are not indigenous to the region, ranging from Border Leicester to Suffolk, are found on Mid Wales farms; but throughout its history, Powys has always been true Sheep Country.

Hafod and hendre

Conditions on the high moorlands have always compelled the migration of livestock to lower land in winter, for only the hardier beasts can survive the mists, rain, snow and ice on the moorlands. The stock carrying capacity of upland pasture, even in the mildest winter, is only a fraction of its capacity in summer. More often than not, the upland farmer does not possess enough lowland to accommodate all his flock and he has to seek pastures elsewhere, outside his holding. The wintering of sheep on lowlands in the English Midlands and the coast of West Wales has always been commonplace.

For those farms with enough low land, it used to be common practice to move flocks to lowland pastures in winter. The sheep were then driven to

The festivities associated with sheep shearing days (left and below) are now becoming a thing of the past

the bare mountains in early spring. Quite often a farmer would have a summer residence (*yr hafod*) in the hills, together with a *hendre* (old township) in the valley. The old system of transhumance (seasonal migration) was highly practised in Mid Wales until the 1950s.

Sheep shearing

Until the introduction of mechanised equipment and the employment of paid, specialised shearing gangs, the annual shearing on Mid Wales farms was a great social occasion. Farmers or their representatives from many miles around saw it as an essential duty to help a neighbour obtain his main source of income – wool. Upland farms depended almost entirely on voluntary co-operation to carry out this vital task. Small-holders and non-agriculturalists had their part to play too, for although they may not have been the owners of flocks themselves, their work on the shearing paid for the right to cut peat on the farmer's mountain, or to plant potatoes on his land. By long established tradition, each farm in a locality was allocated specific days for shearing. If the last Friday in July, for example, was specified as shearing day on a particular homestead, then that day had to be adhered to, with no variation. A week before shearing day, a farmer, often with no assistance but a sure-footed mountain pony and three or four well-trained sheepdogs, gathered his sheep from the unenclosed mountain for washing in a dammed up stream or pond. The actual shearing still takes place in the shearing shed, and the work is carried out on long, narrow benches on which the shearers sit.

Shearing time is still a festive occasion, characterised by a great deal of bantering between the shearers. In the past, it often ended in a feast, with an impromptu concert in the shearing shed. Every locality had its folk singer, story teller and raconteur, who made a point of attending all shearings in a district.

Sheep shearing by hand, as practised on some of the upland farms of Mid Wales, is a vestige of the past when co-operation between farms was a necessity. Alas, the shearing contractor is becoming far more common even on the remotest farms, and the festival atmosphere of the traditional shearing day is rapidly becoming a thing of the past.

Rural Occupations

Until recent times, every rural community in Mid Wales, as in the rest of the Principality, was almost self-sufficient, and only rarely was the countryman forced to go outside his own locality to search for basic resources. In corn mills and tanneries, woollen mills and malting houses, craftsmen processed the products of agriculture while the tools of farming, the furniture and utensils for the home, horse-harness, boots, clogs, ropes and wearing apparel – indeed, everything the community required, could be produced locally. But even if a locality did not possess all the craftsmen it required, there were travelling craftsmen who paid regular visits even to the remotest farmstead on the Beacons.

Since the 1930s great changes have taken place in Mid Wales. The countryman no longer looks towards his own locality for the means of life. The craftsman has lost his place as an essential member of the community, for the products of the industrial regions are within reach of all, while ever-improving transport carries standardised products with more efficiency to the heart of the countryside. In 1900, for example, the old county of Brecknockshire had 22 woollen mills in full production; today only the Cambrian Factory at Llanwrtyd remains. In 1923 there were 31 corn mills in production; today there are hardly any in working order. Blacksmiths and saddlers, wheelwrights and bootmakers, commonplace in Mid Wales 50 years ago, have all virtually disappeared from the rural scene.

Hill country craftsmanship

The fact that Mid Wales has hill regions separating deep valleys has meant that the population has always been concentrated in those valleys. The surrounding hills have always been relatively deserted; and industry in its turn grew up in the valley regions. Those lowland areas had their full quota of craft workshops fulfilling all the needs of the people, and no valley farm was far away from a village or town settlement with its complement of craftsmen. In many cases, the craftsmen who served the farming community were paid, not in cash, but with a proportion of the produce. Thus, for example, Isaac Williams of the Esgair Moel Woollen Mill (now at the Welsh Folk Museum, St Fagans, near Cardiff), in processing wool for local farmers and supplying them with knitting yarn, blankets and cloth, kept a tenth of the fleeces as payment, which he made up into cloth and sold from his market stall at Builth Wells. Country blacksmiths received old iron, bushels of grain and sacks of potatoes in lieu of cash and corn millers kept part of all the grain brought into a mill for processing as their payment for a service.

A wealth of wool

Mid Wales is above all else a sheep producing area, and the extensive sheep runs provided the raw material for the most important and widespread of all industries: wool manufacturing. In the Severn Valley, the makers of woollen goods went beyond the stage of supplying self-sufficient rural communities with their day-to-day requirements, and exported flannel and cloth to all parts of the world. In the heyday of the industry, flannel from the Mid Wales towns of Newtown and Llanidloes clothed the slaves of North America as well as the armies of the Duke of Wellington. Welsh flannel was worn by coal miners and iron-workers and it was deemed to possess 'a peculiar softness of texture which renders it exceedingly well adapted to be worn next to the skin of the most delicate invalid'. Fortunes were made by those concerned with its manufacture. The old county of Montgomeryshire in particular, and the area around Brecon to a lesser extent, possessed all the natural

St Fagans Folk Museum now houses many of the rural workplaces of the past, including a cornmill from Dyfed (above), and a tannery from Rhayader (far right, above and below)

Pleaching – interweaving twigs and branches to make hedges – is one of the highly specialised skills needed in an agricultural community, and practised here by Mr Gwyn Price of Beiligwern

advantages of raw materials and water supply that could have made them into textile manufacturing districts as important as West Yorkshire.

Newtown, the centre of the industry, was known to early 19th-century travellers as 'The Leeds of Wales'; indeed it was truly a 'new town' built round the nucleus of the ancient borough of Llanfair-yng-Nghedewain. The high three or four-floored buildings in the back streets of Newtown, and of Machynlleth and Llanidloes, bear witness to this day of the importance of wool in the history of Powys. A weaving factory occupying the third and fourth floors of a building would stretch over half a dozen or more cottages usually of the back-to-back variety. The factory was usually entered by an outside staircase at the back of the terrace. In many cases the owner of a weaving factory was also the owner of a shop at the end of the row. These shops were the truck shops or 'tommy shops', and weaving masters were adept at by-passing the Truck Acts. The woollen towns of Powys were seed-beds of discontent in the 1840s; but by 1890 the Severn Valley woollen industry had virtually disappeared, due to the competition of a more efficient textile industry in Northern England.

Tanning success

Second in importance to woollen manufacture was that of leather, a well-distributed industry using the skins of Welsh sheep and cattle, and exporting the end-product to other parts of Britain for use in boot and saddle-making. Not only did Powys have the essential raw material, but it also possessed a number of other materials needed for the industry. Bark from the stunted oak trees of the Mid Wales hills was particularly rich in tannin, the chemical agent responsible for the conversion of hide into leather. Welsh mountain sheep provided a plentiful supply of tallow, required for dressing certain types of leather; and clean water from mountain streams ensured that the tanned skins were not discoloured by impurities.

As a result of all these natural advantages, the tanning industry became commonplace in Mid Wales. It was especially important in the market towns – Llanidloes, Newtown, Brecon and Aberystwyth, for instance, where there were ample supplies of cattle and sheep in the hinterland to supply the tanneries with raw materials. One of those tanneries, from the Mid Wales town of Rhayader, is preserved at the Welsh Folk Museum, St Fagans, near Cardiff.

Wooden heart

The Mid Wales valleys, leading into the heart of high moorlands, have always carried heavy growths of timber. Here, where the oak tree predominates, the house-builder's art developed to a very high level. Half-timbered houses were always in demand in this area; they are still found in such valleys as the Severn and Wye, crossing the watershed almost to the shores of Cardigan Bay. Llanidloes in the 18th century was 'a town of houses built with laths and mud filling in the intermediate space of a timber frame'; and Newtown was dominated by the half-timbered style. In the surrounding countryside, cottages and farmhouses, inns and mansions were, until the early 19th century, built with timber frames, with the intermediate spaces infilled with wattle and daub.

Other crafts came into existence in Mid Wales because of the plentiful supply of timber in the valleys. Itinerant clog-sole makers wandered from alder grove to alder grove with a few simple tools, producing soles for the clogging factories of Lancashire and Yorkshire. These craftsmen, living in roughly built huts, were among the most romantic figures of the rural crafts and were still to be seen until 1939. Charcoal burning was also carried out by itinerant workers, especially in the Mynydd Eppynt foothills, and associated with that trade was the production of naphtha oil.

Making paper

One of the least-known of Mid Wales industries was that of paper-making, which developed to a very high level in the valleys around Crickhowell in the late 18th and early 19th centuries. Its success in the remote Grwyne Fawr valley of Brecknock was due to the plentiful supply of pure water, both for driving milling machinery and also for the manufacturing process itself. The mills depended very heavily on adequate supplies of rags collected from all over South Wales. Sorting and rag cutting was a task undertaken by women who, in 1843, were paid an average wage of three shillings. It was very unhealthy work, for rags could carry infectious diseases. Having been sorted and cut, the rags were then stamped to a pulp under the hammers of a mill, and the actual paper was made by hand in wooden moulds. The Grwyne Fawr valley paper mills were particularly famous for producing brightly coloured grocery papers and boards for book binding.

Beer and cider

In the red sandstone soils in the foothills of the Brecon Beacons appreciable quantities of barley were grown in the past. As well as supporting a large number of water-driven corn mills the area possessed a large number of malthouses, where the main ingredient for beer brewing was produced. Throughout the area the remains of malthouses, with perforated floor tiles where barley was dried over wood fires, can still be seen.

Nevertheless, in many parts of Mid Wales, especially towards the eastern boundary, cider was far more important than beer, and orchards containing such varieties of apples as Old Foxwhelp and Redstreak are still to be seen. Dotted all over the countryside are the remains of cider houses which contained horse-driven, stone cider mills for crushing apples. So popular was cider drinking amongst the people of the old county of Brecknock that a temperance leader in the 1930s described it as a 'cider-besotten county'!

The amateur tradition

In addition to the full-time, fully trained craftsmen who practised their trade in permanent workshops, Mid Wales had numerous part-time, amateur workers who served no apprenticeship and hardly even possessed a fully equipped place of work. In an upland district of small, scattered farms, many farmers made their own tools and equipment and did not depend on the services of a specialist professional craftsman. Hand tools and domestic utensils, field gates and fences, animal feeding baskets and transport devices were often produced by hill farmers from the raw materials available in their own immediate localities. In every remote rural community, however, there were always one or two people who were more competent than others in providing the necessities of life. Perhaps one person would be recognised by his neighbours as an efficient maker of straw rope or rush halters, or as a good dry-stone waller or hedger. These were the part-time, semi-professional, though untrained men with dextrous hands that gave them status, in a community which valued manual work.

The amateur craftsman undoubtedly contributed a great deal to the heritage of Mid Wales. In a society where entertainment was at a premium and farmsteads were isolated, many of the inhabitants practised some form of creative craft in their spare time. It was that amateur tradition that gave us exquisitely carved love-spoons and knitting sheaths, patchwork quilts and straw baskets; but of course that leisurely life of the past and its expression in craftsmanship has largely disappeared from the uplands of Central Wales.

Clog-makers provided cheap, tough footwear – still worn in the eisteddfodic clog-dancing contests

BRECON BEACONS
AND MID WALES

Gazetteer

Each entry in this Gazetteer has the atlas page number on which the place can be found and its National Grid reference included under the heading. An explanation of how to use the National Grid is given on page 82.

rediscovered and is now safely embodied in the garden wall of Home Farm.

Abbeycwmhir means 'the Abbey of the Long Valley', and this great building was founded on its present site in 1176, when its first inhabitants were the Cistercian monks from Whitland Abbey in Dyfed. After violent battles it fell into the hands of the powerful Mortimer family and, in 1214, came under the patronage of King John. Torn between loyalties to the Welsh and the English, the Abbey survived another two centuries until 1401, when it is thought to have been sacked by Owain Glyndŵr. The building, which had not been completed, was never fully restored and neither the transept nor the chancel was ever built. The final blow to a building which could have compared with York, Durham and Winchester cathedrals came in 1644, when the Roundheads reduced it to ruins. Many historians believe that the body of the last native Prince of Wales, Llywelyn ap Gruffudd, was carried from the spot where he was killed in 1282, some 12 miles to the south, to be buried in the grounds of the Abbey.

The ancient ruins now lie in a peaceful setting by the Clywedog brook, and there are plans for an interpretative board, improved paths and, eventually, a project to record the distribution of the carved stone from the site – much of which can be seen in Llanidloes church, ten miles to the north-west.

Abergavenny

Map Ref: 93SO2914

This busy market town, often referred to as the 'Gateway to the Vale of Usk', is surrounded by green hills – including the Sugar Loaf and Ysgyryd (Skirrid) Fawr. Although the one way system around the town is somewhat tortuous, there is ample central parking, a small pedestrian area, and several features to make a visit worthwhile.

The castle, of which little now remains, was probably built on the site of a Roman fort and is associated with six centuries of the town's history. It was initially the work of the Norman, Hamelin de Balun (or Ballon) in whose family it remained until 1175 when it passed to William de Braose. This was rather a gruesome period, for his first act was to seek revenge on the Welsh, who had killed his brother-in-law, Henry de Balun. This he did by inviting some of the Welsh chieftains to a banquet on Christmas Day, persuading them to leave their weapons as a gesture of friendship – and then having them brutally murdered. Two hundred years later the Welsh rebel leader, Owain Glyndŵr, was let in through what is now known as 'Traitor's

St Mary's Church in Abergavenny (top) houses the imposing 15th-century wooden figure of the patriarch Jesse (inset)
Above: the remains of Abergavenny castle

Abbeycwmhir

Map Ref: 88SO0571

Situated in the beautiful Clywedog Valley, Abbeycwmhir is a small village with a number of interesting buildings. The old Manor House 'Tŷ Faenor', or 'Devannor' as it is known today, was built in 1680 out of stone from the ruined Abbey, and has a dog-legged staircase of 14th-century origin. The house is not open to the public, being occupied by the Griffiths

family, who have cared for it for nearly two centuries, but from the outside visitors can see where some of the windows were bricked up to avoid the Window Tax in 1696.

Much of the material from the remains of the ancient Abbey was used to construct the village buildings, including, in the 19th century, the present parish church, which has a copy of the typanum from the Abbey with carved stonework depicting the Ascension. Since the church was built, the original typanum has been

Gate' by one of the townswomen. He set fire to Abergavenny and its church, but did not succeed in destroying the castle, which survived until 1645.

Some of the town's existing buildings offer evidence of a varied history: the gatehouse walls are easily accessible, and the barn in Castle Street, built in red sandstone, was once a part of the sheep market in medieval times.

Market Street (the site of 'Traitor's Gate') and Flannel Street – a reminder of the once thriving weaving industry – include fine examples of 17th-and 18th-century buildings while, in Cross Street, the Angel and the King's Head inns point to Abergavenny's past role as a major staging post.

Although St Mary's Church was originally the site of the Benedictine Priory founded by Hamelin de Balun, the present building is 14th-century. It became the parish church during the Dissolution in 1536 and, in spite of suffering desecration at the hands of Cromwell's troops, some of its interesting features have survived, including the 14th-century oak choir stalls, a Norman font and, in the Lewes Chapel, the Jesse Tree – an enormous wooden figure of the patriarch, carved in the 15th century. Many of the castle's occupants were buried in the Priory, the oldest effigy being that of Eva de Braose, wife of the last member of that family to hold the title. Among the tombs is one dated 1273, carved out of a single block of wood and thought to be that of George de Cantelupe, a young knight.

Present day Abergavenny makes ample use of its market place; the large hall houses crafts, produce, general stalls or antiques, depending upon the day; and the town is a favourite base for walkers, fishermen, canal enthusiasts and pony trekkers. There are also plenty of amenities for those who do not wish to stray far, including a leisure centre and museum, and, for anyone needing a guide to its interesting buildings, the Civic Society provides a town trail.

AA recommends:
Hotels: Angel, Cross St, 3-star, *tel.* (0873) 7121
Llanwenarth Arms, Brecon Rd, 2-star, *tel.* (0873) 810550
Restaurant: Bagan Tandoori, 35 Frogmore St, 1-fork, *tel.* (0873) 4790
Guesthouses: Belchamps, 1 Holywell Rd, *tel.* (0873) 3204
Great Lwynfranc, Llanfihangel Crucorney, *tel.* (0873) 890418
Llanwenarth House, Govilon, *tel.* (0873) 830289
Newcourt, Mardy, *tel.* (0873) 2300
Garages: Abergavenny Mtr Co, 9 Monmouth Rd, *tel.* (0873) 2712
W G Lane & Sons, Brecon Rd, *tel.* (0873) 2126
W G Lane & Sons, Ford Depot, Lion St, *tel.* (0873) 2126

Monnow Brec Canal

The Mon and Brec Canal, as it is locally known, was once two waterways – the Monmouthshire Canal and the Abergavenny Canal. These were first opened in the late 18th century, but it was not until 1812 that the two were joined, providing a route from Newport to Brecon. This waterway conveyed iron ore from the south, and brought vital supplies of limestone and coal to the towns on the upper reaches, who had previously paid dearly for such commodities. The economic benefits were noticed as early as 1800, when the last stretch of the second canal was completed. The cheaper transport cut the price of coal in Brecon by half.

Although the barges mainly carried industrial goods, the local farming communities used them to take produce and, sometimes, livestock to the markets; and the canal companies displayed time-tables to encourage passenger traffic. For a while the extended waterway was a busy place; but by the late 19th century railway companies were providing a more efficient means of transport, and by the beginning of World War II the canal had commercial traffic.

Fortunately, the value of this wonderfully scenic waterway was recognised by the Waterways Board and the Brecon Beacons National Park authorities. Due to successful restoration there are now over 30 miles of navigable water from Brecon in the north to Crown Bridge, just below Pontypool, in the south, running through magnificent scenery.

Limekilns at Llangattock and Goytre and old stone warehouses in beautiful settings such as Llanfoist Wharf provide reminders of the canal's commercial history.

There are organised trips and charter craft from the Brecon and Abergavenny area and, for those who wish to 'go it alone', narrow boats and cabin cruisers can be hired from several places, including Gilwern, Govilon, Goytre Wharf and Pencelli. The waterway is a delight for those who enjoy less strenuous navigation, for it has only six locks at its northern end, and 22 miles of it have none at all.

A tow path runs alongside the water for miles; it is possible to cover the whole distance between Brecon and Pontypool by staying overnight at one of the many villages along the way. South of Talybont, the path runs over the top of the Ashford Tunnel – a fact which was appreciated in times past by 'Bob', the boat from Brecon Old Brewery; unobserved, the crew were able to pull up in the tunnel, drain off a quantity of beer from one of the barrels, plug up the hole and replace the hoop, so that no one would know a pint or two had disappeared!

At Pontymoel, near Pontypool, the old canals met, and here Junction Cottage houses a museum covering the waterway's history.

The Mon and Brec Canal's charm has survived changing fashions

ON THE CANAL, BRECON.

Abergwesyn and the Irfon Valley

Map Ref: 87SN8552

The small village of Abergwesyn, west of the A483 and south of Builth Wells, stands at the edge of one of the wildest parts of Mid Wales. With the Irfon, spawning ground of the brown trout, flowing nearby, the village forms a gateway to the impressive mountain road to Tregaron. This was the scene of great activity when the drovers brought their livestock from the west. They started their journey in the early hours of Tuesday or late on Monday night, after the flocks had been assembled from midnight on Sunday, as it was against the law to start herding on the Sabbath. Plodding 14 miles over the mountains, the drovers allowed themselves only three hours' sleep each night. Originally their trek took them through the little village of Beulah, whose name has been given to the famous spotted-face sheep. But after the coming of the railway to Llanwrtyd-Wells, Beulah tended to be by-passed by the drovers who, instead, turned south at Abergwesyn to load their beasts on to the trains.

Not far above Abergwesyn is Wolf's Leap, where a fierce mountain stream rushes through the narrow gorge. From the steep, tortuous zig-zag section of the mountain road known as Devil's Staircase, the Irfon flows down to Llanwrtyd-Wells. Here the valley is rich in wildlife – golden plover and dunlin often breed on the slopes and it is even possible to catch a glimpse of a peregrine falcon, or the famous red kite.

Top : Aberystwyth University – the 'college by the sea'
The ruins of Aberystwyth Castle (above) are set on a lovely headland

Aberystwyth

Map Ref: 86SN5881

This is Cardigan Bay's largest resort, with a shingle beach and a long, wide promenade. At its northern end stands Constitution Hill, with well laid-out paths to the 430ft summit, which, on a clear day, offers wonderful views as far as Snowdon to the north and the Preseli mountains to the south. If this walk seems too daunting, the cliff railway provides a scenic alternative, covering the 900ft journey from the lower station at 4mph, and running daily every ten minutes from Easter to October. When it first opened in 1896, the railway was operated by water balance tanks on the front of the carriages, and although electrified in 1922 and improved upon regularly ever since, the 19th-century design of the carriages has been retained.

A more recent inducement to climb the hill is the Camera Obscura at the top, where a fascinating, enlarged view of the area is projected onto a circular screen in the centre of a dark room. This, too, is open from Easter to October.

Among the traditional entertainments of the north sea-front are a band stand, pier, and, under normal conditions, safe bathing for anyone who doesn't mind struggling over the pebbles to reach the sea.

Just south of the pier, perched on a headland, are the well preserved and easily accessible ruins of the castle, built in 1277 by Edward I and destroyed by Cromwell's forces in 1649. The ruins now form part of a recreation area. Beyond the castle is the harbour, where numerous fishing vessels put out into the bay. Boats for sea fishing may be hired or chartered here.

Aberystwyth is a University town, and the impressive hilltop campus at Penglais offers an Arts Centre with a gallery, theatre and concert hall providing a wide range of entertainment, including Welsh drama and music.

Penglais is also the site of the National Library of Wales, where some of the Principality's greatest library treasures are housed, including old manuscripts like The Black Book of Carmarthen dating back to the 13th century – the oldest intact Welsh manuscript. These are not on public view, but are available by pre-arrangement to researchers. The library also holds a copy of every book published in the United Kingdom for copyright reference.

From Easter to October the Vale of Rheidol Narrow Gauge Railway carries passengers from the main

British Rail Station in Alexandra Road along a delightfully scenic route to Devil's Bridge (see page 48), allowing time to see the magnificent waterfalls before catching the next little steam train back.

Aberystwyth's recreational facilities include golf, bowling, tennis and putting and, for those who do not wish to brave the sea, there is a heated indoor swimming pool at Plas Crug.

AA recommends:
Hotels: Belle Vue Royal, Marine Ter, 2-star, *tel.* (0970) 617588
Cambrian, Alexandra Rd, 2-star, *tel.* (0970) 612446
Conrah, Chaneery, Ffosthydygaled, 3-star Country House, *tel.* (0970) 617941
Court Royale, Eastgate, 2-star, *tel.* (0970) 611722
Four Seasons, 50-54 Portland St, 1-star, *tel.* (0970) 612120
Groves, 42-46 North Parade, 2-star, *tel.* (0970) 617623
Seabank, Victoria Ter, 2-star, *tel.* (0970) 617617
Guesthouses: Glyn-Garth, South Rd, *tel.* (0970) 615050
Llety-Gwyn, Llanbadarn Fawr, *tel.* (0970) 3965
Plas Antaron, Pen Parcau, *tel.* (0970) 611550

Shangri La, 36 Portland St, *tel.* (0970) 617659
Windsor Private Hotel, 41 Queens Rd, *tel.* (0970) 612134
Self Catering: Ael-y-Don Holiday Flats, Cliff Terrace Apartment, *tel.* (097081) 431
Campsite: 'U' Tow Caravans, Aberystwyth Holiday Village, 1-pennant, *tel.* (0970) 4211

Bethlehem and Garn Goch

Map Ref: 88SN6825

This little hamlet on the south-west border of the Beacons National Park takes its name from a Nonconformist chapel. It is of particular interest to philatelists, who can buy first-day covers and specially franked Christmas post bearing the name 'Bethlehem, Llandeilo'.

Overlooking Bethlehem from the south-east, some 700ft up, stand the remains of Garn (or Carn) Goch, a huge Iron Age fort. Among these ruins are narrow postern gates faced with stone slabs, and part of the ramparts which were originally 20ft high and 12ft thick. Strategically placed above the Vale of Tywi, this immense fort was the largest in Wales.

Beulah *see* Abergwesyn

Black Mountains (Mynyddoedd Duon)

Map Ref: 86S022

The Black Mountains area is at the most eastern part of the Brecon Beacons National Park, with Hay-on-Wye at its northern tip and Abergavenny at the south. Of its very few roads, those following the River Honddu (or Hodni) and the Vale of Ewyas are both interesting and scenic, winding past the remains of large religious foundations and little intact ancient churches, including Cwmyoy, Partrishow, Capel-y-ffin and Llanthony Priory, and ending by crossing the impressive Hay Bluff to the north.

On its western side is Maen Llwyd, a standing stone on the south of Pen y Gadair Fawr, north of Crickhowell. Being 1,880ft up, this is the highest standing stone in Wales – but is also somewhat inaccessible!

A glorious view of the Black Mountains can be enjoyed from Mynydd Llangattock

Brecon (Aberhonddu)

Map Ref: 88SO0528

This market town, whose history stretches back to the 12th century and beyond, is situated on the north eastern tip of the Brecon Beacons National Park, where the River Honddu (Hodni) flows into the Usk.

Among the remains of its ancient history is the impressive Priory of St John the Evangelist. Built in the 13th and 14th centuries on the site of a Norman church, this picturesque building became Brecon Cathedral in 1923, and reflects a great deal of the town's history. The grand old protecting wall encircles a good part of it, running up the incline from the Honddu, past the Deanery where Charles I slept in 1645, and round to the old monastic gateway. Inside, the Cordwainers' (or Shoemakers') chapel has a stained-glass window showing three figures, depicting the great families who held the Lordship of Brecknock.

Sights and tastes of Brecon: Welsh Chwisgi (left) and the Zulu War Room at the South Wales Borderers Museum

The Havard Chapel is dedicated to the South Wales Borderers and houses some valuable and interesting gifts, including the oak framed altar and an oil painting by Albani which hangs above it.

The cathedral's choir stalls were not built until 1874 but the tower above them is the oldest part of the building. Looking up, it is possible to see the passages which run through it and which have weakened the structure, making it too dangerous to risk bell-ringing. There is choral evensong on Fridays at 5.45pm and on Sundays at 3.30pm and interesting choral works are performed throughout the year.

St Mary's Church, which stands

The market town of Brecon (Aberhonddu) is set on the beautiful River Usk at its junction with the Honddu (Hodni)

in the centre of the town, is able to provide the bell ringing which the cathedral lacks. The tower, dating from Henry VIII's time, is known as Buckingham Tower after the 2nd Duke of Buckingham, whom Henry had beheaded in 1521.

St Mary's is a good starting point for an exploration of the steep steps and alleyways leading off the narrow pavements. Some of the buildings here date back to the 15th century, and in the High Street is the Sarah Siddons inn – once called the Shoulder of Mutton – where the actress was born in 1755.

A town trail can be bought at the National Park Office in Glamorgan Street, and there is pleasant walking to be had beside the Usk, a river which offers rowing as well as trout and salmon fishing.

The Old County Hall, built in 1842, now houses the Brecknock Museum with its wealth of local history, and within walking distance is an interesting Military Museum, set in the barracks of the South Wales Borderers.

Brecon Castle, built in the time of

Reminders of rural life: a shepherd's smock in the Brecknock Museum in Captain's Walk

William the Conqueror, stands in the grounds of the Castle Hotel, and the ruins, though not safe to explore, are especially impressive at dusk, silhouetted against the Beacons.

Equally atmospheric is Christ College on the other side of the Usk. Founded by Henry VIII in 1541 on the site of a 13th-century friary, most of its present Victorian structure is in Gothic style, but some of the ancient buildings remain and, with permission from the headmaster, it is possible to view them. The chapel and the refectory are particularly interesting.

The town's modern attractions are well worth investigating, too. The annual Jazz Festival is held in August, featuring plenty of top names and a fair amount of ale. However, the town's real home produce is Welsh Whisky, but partakers of this increasingly popular 'Chwisgi' must buy it in pubs, as there are no tours or 'free samples'.

Among Brecon's recreational facilities are two golf courses, bowling greens, tennis courts and an indoor heated swimming pool. The main car park is large and centrally situated alongside the market, and for those who find the climb to the cathedral too arduous, there is

ample parking space just beyond the lych-gate.

AA recommends:

Hotels: Castle of Brecon, Castle Sq, 2-star, *tel.* (0874) 4611
George, George St, 2-star, *tel.* (0874) 3422
Landsdowne, 39 The Watton, 1-star, *tel.* (0874) 3321
Wellington, The Bulwark, 2-star, *tel.* (0874) 5225
Guesthouse: Beacons, 16 Bridge St, *tel.* (0874) 3339
Self Catering: Coach House, Stable Cottage & Court Flat; for bookings Mrs F R Harries, The Court, Cradoc Road, Brecon, Powys *tel.* (0874) 2028
Campsite: Brynich Caravan Park, 3-pennant, *tel.* (0874) 3325

Brecon Beacons National Park Mountain Centre

Map Ref: 88SN9726

Situated off the A470, west of the little village of Libanus, the Mountain Centre, founded with assistance from the Carnegie United Kingdom Trust, was opened in 1966 and covers almost every aspect of the 519 square miles of Brecon Beacons National Park. It stands 1,100ft up on Mynydd Illtud, and is an ideal starting point for visitors planning to explore the National Park. Guided walks can be arranged.

Although over 150,000 people visit the Mountain Centre every year, there is a relaxed, uncrowded atmosphere, and visitors who wander into the main lounge can enjoy the view over the Beacons and examine items which include geological specimens, a relief model of the Park, pictorial illustrations of its history and photographs of its development.

Audio visual facilities and a lecture room are available for groups (although these must be booked well in advance) and an under-cover picnic area provides wash up facilities. The centre closes only on Christmas Day.

Market Days

Market day in Wales is the one day of the week when farming folk are able to get together – not only to buy and sell livestock, but also to take advantage of a time-honoured relaxation in licensing laws, which normally allows the pubs to remain open all day.

The markets held in most towns go back many centuries. A sense of history and long-standing tradition pervades Llandovery's market, for example, enhanced by its location right next to the town's tumbledown medieval castle. Land Rovers may now have replaced the horse and cart, but the same bargaining for the best deal goes on in the sales rings, presided over by the quick-fire – and, to outsiders, largely incomprehensible – verbal dexterity of the auctioneer.

Visitors do not have to understand the ins and outs of bidding to enjoy market days. They can soak up the busy, bustling atmosphere of towns which, for the rest of the week, revert to a fairly peaceful existence. Or they can make the most of the shops which are usually boosted by the market, though some of the smaller venues are purely for livestock sales. All kinds of temporary stallholders move in for the day, selling everything from exotic cheeses to riding tackle, farm implements to craft products.

Locals reckon it's best to arrive early at Abergavenny's weekly market if you want to park anywhere near the town. Brecon

holds two markets each week. And at Llanybydder, near Lampeter, an unusual – and internationally famous – monthly horse fair attracts buyers from all over Britain, and parts of the Continent.

A selection of market days

Monday
Builth Wells
Hay-on-Wye
Llandeilo
Lampeter (fortnightly)
Llanybydder (fortnightly)

Tuesday
Abergavenny
Brecon
Llandovery (fortnightly)
Llangadog (fortnightly)
Tregaron

Wednesday
Sennybridge

Thursday
Knighton
Talybont-on-Usk
Llanwrtyd-Wells (fortnightly and seasonal)
Newtown (fortnightly)
Llanybydder Horse Fair (last Thursday in the month)

Friday
Brecon
Rhayader

Saturday
Caersws (fortnightly and seasonal)
Llanidloes (fortnightly and seasonal)

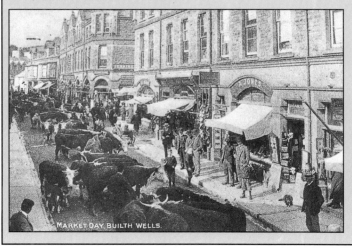

Livestock fills the streets of Builth Wells on market day

Bronllys *see* Talgarth

Builth Wells
(Llanfair-Ym-Muallt)

Map Ref: 88SO0350

This ancient market town on the
banks of the Wye has its roots in
the 11th and 12th centuries, when
the Normans built a castle which
was later partly destroyed by the
Welsh. Although rebuilt by Edward
I, this extremely sturdy fortification
met final destruction in the reign of
Elizabeth I, and nothing now
remains except a few grassy
mounds.

Llanfair-Ym-Muallt means 'St
Mary's in Builth'; and the present
substantial church of that name still
has its 14th-century tower. Standing
in the centre of the town, it is
surrounded by a particularly large
churchyard and it was here that
John Wesley sometimes preached in
the 18th century when the church
could not accommodate all those
who came to hear him.

The death of Prince Llywelyn in
1282 features prominently in
Builth's history. The Prince's ruse
of fixing his horse's shoes
backwards, so that his pursuers
would think he was travelling in the
other direction, failed to save him;
he was betrayed and killed, and his
head displayed in London. A stone
monument, inscribed in Welsh – as
befitting a memorial to the last
native Prince of Wales – has been
erected in Cilmeri, a few miles west
of Builth Wells.

Having suffered terribly in the
Black Death and being almost
completely gutted by fire in 1691,
Builth survived to become a well-
known spa town during the 19th
century, possessing two wells and
sufficient saline water to send
thousands of gallons every year to
nearby Llanwrtyd-Wells. As the
Park Wells were about a mile from
the town, the waters were made
available in the Pavilion on the
Groe in the centre of the town.

Echoes of Builth's Victorian days
can be seen in the old Assembly
Room, built in 1877, which is now ·
the home of the Wyeside Arts
Centre and Cinema.

The old market hall below,
overlooking the river, carries the
Builth Coat of Arms – a white bull
with a red nose – and is a hive of
activity on Mondays, when one can
browse among traditional country
produce and craft stalls before
wandering up the narrow High
Street to the cattle market to see
livestock sold or auctioned. Some
older farmers still observe the
tradition of giving 'luck money' – a
reduction on the agreed price in
private bargains.

Across the river, in the old
county of Radnor, is the village of
Llanelwedd and the site of the
Royal Welsh Showground. For four
packed days every July the Royal

*Father Ignatius (above) established a monastery and church near the little hamlet
of Capel-y-ffin (top) in the late 19th century*

Welsh Agricultural Show is
attended by thousands of visitors
who come, not only to see some of
the best livestock in the country,
but to visit exhibitions, craft stalls,
entertainments and displays.

AA recommends:
Hotels: Caer Beris Manor, Garth Rd,
2-star Country House, *tel.* (0982) 552601
Lion, 2-star, *tel.* (0982) 553670
Guesthouse: Cae Pandy, *tel.* (0982)
553793
Garage: North Rd, *tel.* (0982)
552600(day) 552723(night)

Capel-y-ffin

Map Ref: 88SO2531

Four miles north of Llanthony
Priory, near the hamlet of Capel-y-
ffin, is a building with the
confusingly similar name of
Llanthony Monastery.

This Victorian house of
contemplation was founded by a
remarkable Church of England
clergyman; Joseph Leicester Lyne.
Born in 1837 in Barking, Lyne was
ordained a deacon in 1860 but felt
a call to re-establish monastic life.
By the time he laid the foundation
stone of his monastery in March
1870, the Reverend Lyne had
begun to call himself 'Father
Ignatius of Llanthony Tertia'. He
devoted much of his time to
preaching, going as far as America
in 1890 and used all the money
gained for the monastery and the
nearby church, which was never
fully completed.

Receiving no support from his
own Anglican authorities, Father
Ignatius was finally ordained in the
Monastery church in 1898.

Francis Kilvert, the famous diarist,
records meeting Father Ignatius six
months after the building of the
monastery had been started. He first

caught sight of this cowled monk walking in a field, dressed in 'black Benedictine habit, knotted scourge girdle, a silver cross on the breast and a brazen or gold cross hanging from the rosary of black beads under the left arm'. Kilvert's description is of 'a man of gentle simple kind manners with a fine brow and saintly face', who was 'excitable and entirely possessed of one idea'.

The monastery was, alas, destined to fail, for after its founder's death in Camberley, Surrey, in 1908, and in spite of the efforts of Father Asaph Harris who succeeded him, Llanthony Tertia soon ran out of funds. It was used from time to time by the Caldey Island Benedictine monks, who were unable to do more than send a resident caretaker there.

The building, now privately owned, still has a chapel where Mass may be said; but the monastery was bought, as a dwelling, by the sculptor Eric Gill in 1924 and is still occupied by his family.

Anyone visiting the church should not miss St Mary's Church at Capel-y-ffin, where a gallery runs along the south and west walls of the tiny building. Examination of the east and north windows will reveal that they are not in fact stained glass but coloured paper. Across the churchyard on the eastern side is the Baptist Chapel, once a schoolhouse for this tiny community, which has three religious houses within a stone's throw of one another.

Carreg Cennen Castle

Map Ref: 91SN6619

Carreg Cennen Castle is probably the most impressively sited ruin in South Wales. Standing on the edge of a sheer limestone crag, 300ft above the Cennen Valley with magnificent views across the Beacons, it has a brooding, medieval atmosphere. Part of the mixed woodland below is managed as a local nature reserve.

Built around the 12th century by Lord Rhys of Dinefwr on an existing fortification which probably went back to Roman times, the present castle had 200 to 300 years' working history, during which it changed hands several times, enduring the squabbles and skirmishes among the Welsh and English.

During one decade in the late 13th century, following its initial capture by Edward I, possession and repossession of Carreg Cennen took place four or five times until, having been rebuilt, it was inherited by John of Gaunt in 1362, passing to Henry Bolingbroke, who later became Henry IV. After withstanding a year long siege by Owain Glyndŵr some forty years later, the great walls were ultimately conquered. Having been surrendered by the Lancastrians without a fight during the Wars of the Roses, it was demolished in 1462 to prevent its use as a robbers' shelter. This sorry task took 500 men with picks and crowbars to accomplish. Fortunately it wasn't pulled down to the ground, and the substantial ruins still give a good idea of the original layout – including a complicated barbican and an entrance constructed so that no one could gain direct access.

One of the main features of Carreg Cennen is a natural underground hollow thought to have been used in prehistoric times and reached from inside the castle through a passage over 200ft long. This eerie entrance is carved into the face of the cliff, and the slits in its walls give only a little light. Explorers should tread warily in order not to disturb Owain Lawgoch (Owain of the Red Hand) who, it is said, has been sleeping in the cave with his men for nearly 700 years, waiting for the trumpet which will summon them to chase the Saxons out of Wales.

An interesting addition to the castle's attractions is the Rare Breeds Centre, where one can see cattle, including Longhorn and Shaggy Highland, and primitive breeds of sheep, as well as pigs, poultry and old farm machinery. The Centre has refreshments, a children's adventure area and picnicking facilities.

The nearby Trapp Art and Crafts Centre, housed in converted barns, has an art gallery on the first floor, a craft shop and tea rooms. In the holiday season visitors can enjoy demonstrations by blacksmiths, woodturners, sculptors and carvers, along with other intriguing exhibitions.

Carreg Cennen Castle dominates the glorious Cennen Valley

Castell Dinas

Map Ref: 88SO1730

The remains of the ancient fort of Castell Dinas occupy a commanding position. They stand at nearly 1,500ft on an exposed solitary site, looking down on fields but over-shadowed by the formidable Black Mountains to the east.

Although a medieval castle was also built on the site, there is little remaining of the stone stronghold and it is the Iron Age hill fort which is still in evidence. The ramparts, steep sides and great ditches are still well defined, and it is difficult to believe that they were probably built as early as 500BC.

Cilycwm

Map Ref: 87SN7540

In the days when the cattle were driven across the hills on their long journey to England, this little village, reached over the 16th-century bridge of Dolauhirion, was a collecting place; and the cobbled water courses can still be seen in front of the houses, ready to provide a drink for the livestock.

Cilycwm is not as busy as it was in those days, but it is still an attractive village, with the Gwenlais running alongside on its way to the Tywi. Its church, with yews of ancient origin, has several wall paintings, including one of a skeleton on the west wall, dating from the 15th century. Once a strong centre of Welsh Methodism, the chapel is thought to have been one of their earliest meeting places. This little place of worship is closely connected with its neighbour, the 150-year-old Neuadd Inn, which stands right next to the graveyard. Situated to the east of Caeo Forest and south of the 1,500ft Mynydd Mallaen, Cilycwm is right on the edge of the wild region and forms a convenient starting point for a visit to the Llyn Brianne Dam and Reservoir (see page 59).

Eighteenth-century Ash Brook House was the home of Francis Kilvert, who chronicled the country life around Clyro in the late 19th century

Clyro

Map Ref: 88SO2143

This pleasant village boasts a history dating back to the days of the Romans, who used it as a stopping-off point *en route* to the west. Although little remains of the nearby castle, built by William de Braose, the Normans were also in occupation in the area.

The village's main claim to fame is its connection with the well known diarist, Reverend Francis Kilvert, curate of Clyro from 1865 until 1872. He lived at Ash Brook House, opposite the Baskerville Arms, and in 1870 started the journal which is now regarded as one of the most charming and informative records of rural Victorian life. These accounts of his

Adelina Patti

Adelina Patti was born in Madrid, of Italian parents, in 1843. She bought the Craig-y-nos estate at the height of her career in 1878, and soon set about extending and improving it, bringing all possible civilised comforts to her remote Welsh retreat. These soon attracted a dazzling cosmopolitan array of house guests, including royalty. She developed the grounds for shooting and fishing, and within the castle even installed a tiny private theatre in classical style. At the theatre's official opening on 'the glorious twelfth' in 1891, acts from *La Traviata* and *Faust* were performed. From then on, Patti continued to entertain her guests in grand style, even allowing the 'Welsh peasantry' into the gallery during performances.

Patti's second husband, the French tenor Ernest Nicolini, died in 1898. A year later, in her mid-fifties, she married 29-year-old Baron Rolf Cederstrom. By the turn of the

The great opera singer Adelina Patti brought high society to her home in Craig-y-nos

century, her great years of entertaining – and those of Craig-y-nos – were over. Sale of the costly estate was contemplated, but did not take place until after her death in 1919.

journeys around the countryside and encounters with the inhabitants filled more than 22 notebooks, but it was not until about 1939 that they were published, in three volumes.

Not far from Clyro is the village of Llowes, whose churchyard is the setting for a fine Celtic cross, 'Great Cross of St Meilig'. Dating from around AD600, this 11ft long structure weighs three and a half tons and is incised with 7th- and 11th-century crosses. Further out into 'Kilvert Country', to the south west, is Glasbury and Maesyronnen Chapel which, founded in 1696, is the oldest Nonconformist meeting house in Wales.

AA recommends:
Hotel: Three Cocks, 2-star, *tel.* (04974) 215
Guesthouses: Ffordd Fawr Farm, Glasbury, *tel.* (04974) 332
Old Gwernyfed Country Manor, Three Cocks, *tel.* (04974) 376

Craig Cerrig-gleisiad Nature Reserve

Map Ref: 88SN9621

The Old Red Sandstone craig, or rock, from which this 156-acre nature reserve takes its name stands at a height of 2,000ft. This is a favourite haunt of many birds which prefer stark mountain terrain,

including the noisy black raven, and is also the home of rare alpine and arctic plants (see page 11).

Although there are public rights of way across the reserve, the land is privately owned and anyone wishing to stray from these must obtain permission from the Nature Conservancy Council at Plas Gogerddan, Aberystwyth (see *Directory*).

Craig y Cilau Nature Reserve

Map Ref: 92SO1815

This National Nature Reserve, covering 157 acres and established in 1959, can be reached by a track leading off the minor road heading westwards out of Llangattock. There is another road, to the eastern hill of the reserve, but this entails negotiating narrow winding lanes with some very steep inclines.

Part of Craig y Cilau reaches a height of 1,500ft, overlooking the River Usk, and is of great interest to botanists, who come to see such rarities as the lesser whitebeam. Cavers are attracted to the Agen Allwedd underground system – at some 12 miles long, one of the longest in Britain to have a single entrance. Although visitors may wander at will on the path crossing the park, the cave itself is closed off and entrance restricted to caving clubs.

Craig-y-nos Country Park

Map Ref: 91SN8415

Opened in 1976, the delightful park of Craig-y-nos is in a beautiful setting under Craig-y-nos (Rock of the Night), from which it takes its name. Its woodlands, streams and walks cover about 40 acres, and the River Tawe is joined by the Llynfell, flowing through the centre. Among the man-made features are a lake, complete with island, and an ornamental pond.

The land once formed the pleasure gardens attached to Craig-y-nos 'Castle' – really a Gothic style country house, which belonged to the famous opera singer, Adelina Patti (see panel).

The 'castle', which can be glimpsed from the Park, became a sanatorium in 1919, and has recently been bought by a local businessman and opera lover, who has promised that the little theatre will continue to be made available to local drama societies and groups; although the fate of the house itself is not clear.

Little remains of Castell Dinas – once the site of an Iron Age fort and a medieval castle

Crickhowell

Map Ref: 92SO2118

The name of this interesting little market town by the side of the River Usk is derived from the Iron Age fort, Crug Hywel (Howell's Cairn). Set on the summit of Table Mountain, some 1,481ft up, this ancient stronghold overlooks the town from the north and is said to be the home of the 9th-century king Hywel Dda, the first to lay down laws for the government of the Welsh.

The buildings in Crickhowell span some seven centuries, the oldest being Alisby's Castle, whose ruins stand in a public park alongside the main road. Built in 1272 by the Norman, Sir Grimbald Pauncefort, it changed hands several times, falling on one occasion into those of Roger Mortimer. Its name derives from his ally, Alisby, who was given the castle as thanks for obtaining Mortimer's release from the Tower of London. The fortifications were attacked, as were so many, by Owain Glyndŵr, and after further collapse in 1917 little is left other than the gatehouse tower, with curtain wall and portcullis gate.

The streets of the town are full of interesting architecture. The barn in New Road was once a mill for the flourishing flannel industry; one of the Crickhowell looms is now housed in St Fagan's Folk Museum in Cardiff.

On the junction of the A40 and New Road stands Porth Mawr, the great gateway which is all that remains of Cwrt-y-Carw, home of the Herbert family, built during the

A mathematical mystery? Crickhowell bridge has 12 arches on one side – and 13 on the other . . .

reign of Henry VIII. Further along the main road is Gwern-vale, now a hotel, but originally the home of Sir George Everest. Alongside this building is a Neolithic burial chamber, about 4,000 years old.

Crickhowell's varied architecture ranges from fine Georgian buildings, including Latham House and Ivy Tower in the High Street, to the ancient Bear Hotel with its cobbled stone forecourt, right on the side of the main road.

One of the town's most intriguing constructions is the bridge over the Usk, known to have been in existence in 1538 but rebuilt in 1706. Built in local stone, it can be a little disconcerting, having 13 arches on one side and 12 on the other – the result of alterations made in 1830.

Crickhowell's present church, dedicated to the 9th-century St Edmund, dates mainly from the 14th century and has a carved 1668 font, fine stained-glass windows and a carved reredos behind the altar, depicting The Last Supper. Although the attractive spire is well worth a viewing, its rebuilding in 1861 was a matter of some local controversy, due to the cost involved.

For the more adventurous visitors, Crickhowell offers a hang-gliding centre among other sporting activities; but others may be content to follow the town trail or visit the hand-made furniture workshops, 100yds off the main road.

AA recommends:

Hotels: Bear, 2-star, *tel.* (0873) 810408
Gliffaes, 2-star Country House, *tel.* (0874) 730371
Restaurant: Glen-y-Dwr, Brecon Rd, 1-fork, *tel.* (0873) 810756
Guesthouse: Dragon Country House Hotel, High St, *tel.* (0873) 810362
Campsite: Riverside Caravan & Camping

Park, 1-pennant, *tel.* (0873) 810397
Garages: Granada Pk Mtrs, Llangattock, *tel.* (0873) 810304
New Road, New Road, *tel.* (0873) 810045

Cwmyoy Leaning Church

Map Ref: 89SO2923

Motorists travelling along the B4423 can be forgiven for thinking they have over-indulged at the local inn when sighting Cwmyoy church about a mile to the east. The whole building leans at an extraordinary angle, and is certainly worth a detour to explore more closely, making use of a small parking space by a nearby farm gate (see Walk 1, p102).

This little medieval church gradually tilted further and further up the hillside as subsidence took place. It had been built below the site of an old landslide, and diagrams tracing the subsidence are now displayed in the porch. So crazy is the angle of the church that the effect inside is quite disconcerting, completely upsetting all sense of balance.

The rough stone cross just inside the door, dating from the 9th or 10th century, was stolen from the church about ten years ago but luckily retrieved by a woman who spotted it in an antique dealer's window in London. Its return was the cause of some embarrassment; nobody had noticed that this ancient and heavy piece of stonework was missing!

Cwmystwyth

Map Ref: 87SO7874

Approaching Devil's Bridge from the scenic B4574, there suddenly

appears an impressive glimpse of the area's past. One of the largest lead mining centres in Wales, the Cwmystwyth mines were worked by the Romans, and by the monks from nearby Strata Florida in the 14th century; and, during the 17th and 18th centuries were one of the most advanced systems in Europe, producing both silver and lead. The remains, which include a dressing mill and turbine house, are quite awesome, set in an isolated area and probably best seen from the roadside.

The mines lie east of the little village of Cwmystwyth, which means Ystwyth Valley, and from there one can drive, via Devil's Bridge, to Ponterwyd on the A44 where the Llywernog Silver Lead Mine Museum takes visitors through the history of the local industry. The 'Miner's Trail' offers a look at the working water mills and exhibitions and 'Balcombe's Level', which can be a little damp.

Dan-yr-Ogof Caves

Map Ref: 91SN8316

The tour of these splendid caves starts from a point 800ft above sea level, and involves a fascinating

Sightseers come in all shapes and sizes . . . one of the residents of Dan-yr-Ogof's Dinosaur Park

journey across bridges and up steps. This takes in features such as the Frozen Waterfall, Wolf's Head and Flitch of Bacon, and enters the Dagger Chamber. If there has been heavy rain, the river can seem alarmingly close!

The caves, considered even now to be only half explored, were entered by the Morgan brothers, Jeff and Ashwell, in 1912, and the 1912 Door commemorates their discovery. The Show Cave was opened to the public in 1939, closing after a short period to store 5,000 tonnes of TNT. It was not until 20 years later that the caves re-opened, in 1964, and since then Dan-yr-Ogof has gone from strength to strength, winning eight awards. One of these was for the Bone Cave, where the life of the inhabitants of 3,000 years ago is examined.

While exploring Dan-yr-Ogof, now recognised as a Site of Special Scientific Interest, there is also an opportunity to visit the life-size Dinosaur Park, and to use the artificial ski slope; and for those who prefer more leisurely pursuits, the site has a museum, restaurant, shop, information centre and picnicking and fishing facilities.

Devil's Bridge

Map Ref: 86SN7376

These dramatic waterfalls, set in magnificent woodland, are the meeting place of the rivers Rheidol and Mynach, and are best seen from below. This means descending into the depths of the gorge where, from the little bridge at the bottom, one can watch the lovely cascades of water. The descent, known as Jacob's Ladder, has 91 steps and is extremely steep; the recommended time of ¾ hour should perhaps be taken as a minimum.

Devil's Bridge is one of three built over the River Mynach, which contributes 300ft of water to the falls. The bridge is thought to have been constructed by Cisterican monks from Strata Florida, eight miles away, and is known to have been in existence in the 12th century.

An old Welsh tale claims that the Devil built the bridge after striking a bargain with an elderly woman whose cow was stuck on the other side. According to their bargain the Devil was to have the first creature to cross the river, but his designs were thwarted when the old woman threw some food over, inticing a starving dog to cross first. A second bridge was built higher up in 1753 and the third, constructed of iron, was completed in 1901.

Railway enthusiasts are attracted by the narrow gauge track which terminates at Devil's Bridge station. It takes the steam locomotives an hour to cover the 12-mile journey, which entails a 680ft climb to the top of the gorge and a halt to take on water. There is a splendid view to be had from the north facing windows of the train where passengers can look down to the Cwm Rheidol Reservoir and see the sites of the old zinc and lead mines. The railway was built in 1902 to carry these commodities to the ships at Aberystwyth, but it was the tourist trade which eventually determined the location of the station at such a picturesque spot.

Devil's Staircase
see Abergwesyn

Dinas RSPB Reserve

Map Ref: 87SN7846

Dinas is a cone-shaped hill situated where the valleys of the Tywi and Doethie rivers meet, and is translated as 'fort' or 'citadel'. As the name suggests, there was probably much more activity in the area centuries ago than its present scenic isolation would imply.

Owned by the RSPB since 1968, the Dinas Nature Reserve covers 101 acres and can be explored by a

Garreg Ddu: man-made beauty

footpath which skirts the hill. This is accessible from the car park and information centre via a ¼ mile wooden boardwalk across the bog which leads along the path of the Tywi gorge. Most visitors can hope to see the famous red kite here, and although it no longer nests in the reserve, it often flies over the valley in the winter and spring. There are also signs that the red squirrel, ousted by its grey cousins for 20 years, is beginning to make its home in the local conifer forests.

Dolaucothi Mines
see Pumsaint

Elan Valley

Map Ref: 87SN96

Frequently referred to as the Lakeland of Wales, this beautiful region has some of the area's most magnificent scenery. Approaching from Rhayader along the B4518, one can look down and see, on the left, little Elan Village, built specially to accommodate the employees of the huge Elan Estate. It is then worth stopping at the Visitor Centre for information about this vast area and a look at the audio visual theatre and exhibitions.

It is usual to drive clockwise around the reservoirs (see Tour 1) having made a lefthand detour to the most recently constructed – the Claerwen. Opened in 1952, this dam stands in splendid isolation, towering 184ft above the river bed. It is the largest of the reservoirs, capable of holding 10,620 million gallons of water.

The first reservoir, crossed by Garreg Ddu viaduct, is called Caban-coch. With a capacity of 7,800 million gallons, its depths are thought-provoking, for some of the area's thousand or so workers occupied houses which were eventually submerged here. Among

these was 'Cwm Elan' which belonged to the uncle of the poet, Shelley. Shelley's house, Nantgwyllt, was also destined for submersion, and when the water is low its garden walls can still be seen, about a mile beyond Garreg Ddu. It is popularly supposed that this lost mansion inspired Francis Brett Young's novel *The House Under the Water*. All in all, some 18 farmhouses, a school and a church were lost beneath the water, but one of the 'long houses' was salvaged from the Claerwen reservoir for display at St Fagan's Folk Museum in Cardiff.

The next reservoir, Pen-y-garreg, is easily identified by its island, which was accessible over dry land during the drought. At the approach, a very small parking area affords a magnificent view and there is a path running down to the bottom of the dam, close enough to be splashed by the water.

There is also limited room to park by Craig Goch, the last in the chain, over which one can walk; an odd experience when the water is pouring over beneath.

After leaving Craig Goch, the road leads into vast moorland populated by some of the area's 45,000 sheep, and continues over Pont ar Elan, a small bridge leading to the old drovers' road to Aberystwyth.

AA recommends:
Hotel: Elan Valley, Elan Valley, 2-star, *tel.* (0597) 810448

The llwy caru – love spoon – was a betrothal gift involving painstaking work by the carver

carver – and to the endless, dark, winter evenings he had to fill. Wherever possible, only a single block of wood was used. Out of this was fashioned a spoon, purely non-functional in design, decorated with elaborate motifs, interlocking chain links, slotted handles, ingenious features and minute details, and sometimes even incorporating more than one spoon bowl. The more elaborate the design, the greater the fervour of the carver's passion.

Although historians speculate over the precise symbolic meaning of the love spoon, it was probably used to 'break the ice' – the acceptance or refusal of the spoon by the girl would indicate if a courtship should lead to betrothal or not. Although the official relationship between the sexes must have been a highly formal affair, a study of love spoons reveals some quite forthright statements about prospective marriages. Certain motifs are supposed to relate to symbols of affection and fertility. Hearts, locks, keys, anchors, bells, vine and bay leaves were carved on the spoon, and in some parts of Wales the number of little wooden balls moving freely within the cavity of the spoon's rect-angular or circular handle is sup-posed to represent the number of children that the young man wished for – after marriage, of course.

One of the finest displays of love spoons in Wales can be seen in the Brecknock Museum, Brecon, where over 20 examples are on display.

Love Spoons

Would you prefer a wooden spoon to an engagement ring? In the rural Wales of old, love spoons were used as symbols of betrothal, and the carving of wooden spoons was a popular pastime on Welsh farms during the long winter nights. From the 17th to the end of the 19th century, the tradition of presenting a girl with an intricately carved, highly decorative spoon as a token of love was widespread throughout the rural communities.

Love spoons, which come in a variety of shapes and sizes, are a testament to the patient skills of the

The Gap Road and the Neuadd Reservoirs

Map Ref: 92SO0318

The Gap route lies to the north of the Neuadd reservoirs, cousins of the larger waters of Pontsticill below. This throughway, nearly 2,000ft high, crosses the heights of the Brecon Beacons, and is thought by some to have been a Roman road leading northwards to Y Gaer, the great fort which was the nucleus of the network of Roman tracks (see page 16).

Some believe that the fort's south-eastern traffic would have travelled via the Usk Valley, but doubts about its origin do not detract from the beauty and excitement of this rough red path as it clings to the mountainside.

Garn Goch *see* Bethlehem

Hay Bluff (main picture) recalls the Norman word haie – hedge – as does Hay-on-Wye (left and far right). The name Gospel Pass dates from the Third Crusade

Garwnant Forest Visitor Centre

Map Ref: 92SO0013

Lying on the southern edge of the Brecon Beacons National Park, the Garwnant Forest Visitor Centre is pleasantly situated, with a verandah overlooking the Llwyn-On reservoir. Carefully maintaining the character of the old farm buildings from which it was built, the centre offers a wealth of information on the surrounding forests: It provides a lecture room, slide shows, models, photographs, and a children's adventure playground.

Much of the surrounding forest was created by the Forestry Commission, who started planting in the Talybont Valley area in 1937 and have now covered over 10,000 acres with trees. The walks here are not confined to avenues of conifers, however, but meander alongside the stream among pleasantly varying surroundings. The forest in which the Garwnant Centre stands, Coed Taf Fawr, was an indirect result of the 19th-century cholera epidemic when new reservoirs were built to supply clean water to South Wales, and trees were planted to shelter the catchment areas.

Now some of the plantations are mature enough to be felled, and serve a practical purpose as well as giving pleasure to many visitors.

Hay Bluff and Gospel Pass

Map Ref: 88SO2436, 88SO2335

Pen-y-Beacon, locally known as Hay Bluff, is the northern-most tip of the Black Mountains range, 2,219ft high and soaring above the Offa's Dyke Path, which here reaches the highest point in its 168-mile route through the length of Wales.

From the narrow road skirting the Bluff to the west, there are breathtaking views right over Hay town to the Wye Valley, and across to the hills of Radnor Forest and Mynydd Eppynt.

To the south, on a minor road which winds its way up through the Vale of Ewyas, is Bwlch-yr-Efengyl, a stretch of road rising to 1,778ft and known in English as Gospel Pass. This name is thought to have originated in the beginning of the

12th century when, during the Third Crusade, Giraldus Cambrensis, then Archdeacon of Brecon, travelled through the Vale of Ewyas, preaching and raising funds for the Crusade.

Hay-on-Wye (Y Gelli)

Map Ref: 88SO2242

The Hay, as it was once called, is a border town in more than one sense. It sits both on the north-east border of the Brecon Beacons National Park, and on the county border, with Powys to its west and Hereford and Worcester to the east.

Like many townships, this busy centre's origins are focused around the castle, whose turbulent history is typical of the Welsh border fortifications.

Originally, there was a small castle near the parish church, but this was replaced by a much larger, Norman building in around 1200. In the mid-17th century, a local family, the Gwynns from Trecastle, built a mansion within the old walls and the building was leased until Victorian times, when it was occupied by the clergy of Hay. In the 20th century two fires broke out – one in 1939 and another in 1977 when the castle was owned by Richard Booth. This colourful personality created considerable publicity by declaring himself 'King of the Castle' and Hay an independent town, and founded the famous secondhand book centre in 1961. The town is now reputed to house the largest collection of used books in the world, with over a dozen shops scattered around the various streets.

Unfortunately, little remains of the medieval walls of 1236, and many of the town's old buildings have been renovated in a way which hides their ancient timbers; but the 17th-century frontage of The Bear is worth a look, and the 16th-century Three Tuns still has a mounting block outside.

In the library is an old iron wheel from the tram track, reflecting the transport problems of the past. In the early 18th century, coal was brought by canal barge as far as Brecon and Abergavenny and conveyed the rest of the way to Hay by cart. Later a tramway was built from Brecon to Hay.

South, on the B4350, lies Old Gwernyfed Manor House, built on the site of a medieval mansion in 1633 by Sir Henry Williams, Court Physician to James I. Among the stories attached to the old house is one that it is cursed because the centre porch – older than the actual house – was taken from Llanthony Abbey after the Dissolution. The inscriptions placed seemingly at random on the pillars of the old banqueting room are believed to be a message to Prince Rupert from Charles I, instructing him to take his son to France, should he be defeated by the Parliamentarians.

AA recommends:
Hotels: Crown, Broad St, 1-star, *tel.* (0497) 820435
Kilvert Country, The Bull Ring, 2-star, *tel.* (0497) 821042
Olde Black Lion, Lion St, 2-star, *tel.* (0497) 820841
Guesthouses: York House, Hardwick Rd, Cusop, *tel.* (0497) 820705
Self Catering: Rose Cottage, Bronydd, for bookings Mrs M Law, Cabalva Farmhouse, Whitney-on-Wye, Herefordshire, *tel.* (04973) 324
Campsite: Hollybush Inn, 1-pennant, *tel.* (04974) 371

Irfon Valley *see* Abergwesyn

Knighton (Trefyclawdd or Trefyclo)

Map Ref: 89SO2872

Set 600ft above sea level alongside the English border, Knighton qualifies as a true Marcher town. As its Welsh name, which means 'Town on the Dyke' suggests, it stands directly upon Offa's Dyke – the only town to do so.

Occupation of the area took place long before this earthwork was built in the 8th century; there is evidence of Stone and Bronze Age man. Among the remains of nearby forts to the north east is Caer (fort) Caradoc, which takes its name from a Silurian chief who is thought to have fought his final battle here.

The layout of the town stems from the original castle, running down the hill past the clock tower around which the market stalls are set. The town is crammed with interesting features, including The Narrows, a street dating from Tudor days, where the houses are dovetailed into one another. In the past one side was called Salutation Inn, having been a long single building. Nearby, the Old House now has some 17th-century features, but was originally a medieval cruck house, with no chimney – just a hole in the roof to let the smoke out. It is thought to be the earliest of its type to be found in a town.

Knighton's market days on Thursdays are, fortunately, a different affair from the relatively recent practices of 150 years ago, when a wife could be bought for one shilling, the women being led in on a rope like cattle. One husband

was heard to say that he would give the purchaser the rope as well, a gesture which presumably clinched the deal.

Rebuilt in 1877 on the site of a Norman church, the present St Edward's, the only church in Wales so dedicated, retains its medieval tower with timbered belfry, where the ancient custom of ringing in the New Year is still followed. The ringing of another sort of bell is

common in Knighton when the Town Crier, a colourful figure in full regalia, strides up and down, holding forth in stentorian tones.

Among other places worth a visit in the town are the Offa's Dyke Heritage Centre in West Street, and nearby Jacket's Well, once known as St Edward's Well, where the water is said to be good for sprains and similar ailments. Its present name derives from the Welsh word for health: 'iechyd'.

AA recommends:
Guesthouses: Heartsease, *tel.* (05474) 220
Milebrook House, Mile Brook, *tel.* (0547) 528631
Self Catering: Cefnsuran, Llangunllo, *tel.* (054781) 219
Upper Bailey Farm, bookings to White Anthony Bungalow, *tel.* (0547) 528405

Lampeter (Llanbedr Pont Steffan)

Map Ref: 86SN5748

Lampeter stands in the Upper Teifi Valley, with the river running nearby, and has a neat 19th-century image. But despite the Victorian town hall and St Peter's Church, rebuilt in 1869, this was a market town as long ago as the 15th century. For hundreds of years, livestock was sent across the drovers' road to be sold in England. The Ram Inn, one mile to the east, was one of the original hostelries used by those undertaking the journey.

One of the town's most impressive buildings is St David's University College, the third oldest in England and Wales. Now a constituent of the University of Wales, the college was founded in

Main picture: Knighton
Inset: window in Lampeter church dating from about 1901

1823 by Bishop Burgess for the education of the clergy and granted a charter to confer Bachelor of Arts degrees in 1863. In the college grounds are the remains of an old castle mound, thought to have been built by King Stephen; and the college itself is open to the public.

During the Civil War, Lampeter was torn when two of its most influential families supported the opposing sides. The Evans family of Peterwell supported the Parliamentary forces, and the Lloyds of Maesyfelin raised their banner for the Royalist cause. A local tale tells of one of the Lloyds a century later who, annoyed that he was unable to purchase some land, lowered a ram down the chimney of the unfortunate owner and, in his capacity of magistrate, had him executed for sheep stealing!

Nearby Cellan, said to be the last place in Britain where a beaver was caught, now has a better claim to fame: it's the home of an unusual exhibition of over 400 model aircraft, representing different types used by the RAF and Fleet Air Arm, together with many military vehicles and figures. This fascinating private collection at Brooklands is open on Wednesdays from July to September, when the proceeds from the small entrance fee are donated to the RAF Benevolent Fund.

AA recommends:
Hotels: Black Lion Royal, 2-star, *tel.* (0570) 422172
Falcondale, 3-star, Country House, *tel.* (0570) 422910

Garage: Service, North Rd, *tel.* (0570) 422549

A dramatic view of the Black Mountain's long moorland

Llanddeusant and the Black Mountain

Map Ref: 87SN7724, 91SN71

Llanddeusant's tiny church is thought to have been built on the site of an early monastery. Evidence of its ancient origins comes in the form of a cross slab found nearby, and possibly dating from the 7th century.

The hamlet itself is a good starting point for explorers of Bannau Sir Gaer, or the Carmarthen Fans as they are called in English. It is one of several little places joined together by a spidery network of lanes, scattered around the north of the Black Mountain. This range, stretching northwards from Brynamman, is crossed by the scenic A4069, which climbs 1,500ft out of the valleys. Once a turnpike road in the late 18th century, this route carried the lime from farming communities up the Tywi Valley.

Apart from a few isolated tracks, little crosses the remote mountain east of the A4069 except the River Twrch, whose name recalls the Welsh stories of the 'Mabinogion', which tell of the boar 'Twrch Trwyth', hunted in vain by King Arthur.

Offa's Dyke

Built in the 8th century by Offa, King of Mercia, this boundary between England and Wales is virtually the same as it was over 1,000 years ago, following the natural contours of the landscape and stretching through the entire length of Wales. The great 12ft ditch, from which a wall of equal height was thrown up, was designed to mark out the boundary of the King's lands; but it is thought that its northern end was incomplete when he was killed in the Battle of Rhuddlan in AD796. It now finishes at Gop Hill, just south of

The commemorative stone of Offa's Dyke near Knighton

Prestatyn; the latter coastal town is believed to have been Offa's ultimate goal.

The Offa's Dyke Path was officially opened in 1971, its 168 miles tracing the line of the Dyke wherever possible. It does, however, make interesting detours over hills, crossing 14 miles of the high isolated area between Llanfihangel Crucorney and Hay-on-Wye. Here the hills and rivers were probably sufficient boundaries, and there is no Dyke to follow.

For a view of the Dyke without the walk, the section north of Knighton, where it runs exposed across bare land, is considered one of the best. The path itself is well marked, but crosses very varied terrain, from the pastoral lowlands to rugged hill country, and walkers are advised not to cross the latter regions on their own, or if bad weather threatens.

Knighton, the only town to stand right on the Dyke, is the site of the Offa's Dyke Heritage Centre, set in pleasant parkland by the River Teme, where the route and its history can be studied on audio visual facilities, and in the exhibition area.

Beautifully set in the Tywi Valley, Llandeilo (right) has a 700-year history. Lloyds Bank (below) was set up by a Llandovery drover

Llanddew

Map Ref: 88SO0530

Llanddew's Church of St David, which has a charming squat appearance and is equally attractive inside, stands on one of the most ancient sites in the region, dating back to AD500. The present building is thought to be the oldest church in what was the old county of Brecknock, having a 12th-century chancel, transepts with small arched entrances, an interesting trefoil-headed priest's doorway and a very ancient font.

Among the other interesting features is the pulpit, dedicated to the 12th-century churchman and writer, Giraldus Cambrensis, who lived in Llanddew when he was Archdeacon of Brecon (see page 56). The ruins of the palace which he occupied, now the property of the Bishop of St David's, are in the grounds of the vicarage.

Llanddewi-Brefi

Map Ref: 87SN6655

Nestling among the hills, south west of Tregaron, this village dates back to the 6th century and St David, after whom it was named. The large church, with its modern sculpture of the Welsh saint within, is a predominant feature, standing on a mound which may once have been an old place of worship. An alternative explanation for the hillock is given in the legend that so many people came to hear St David speak at the Synod of Brefi that the earth rose up beneath him.

The name of the village is another source of legend. 'Llanddewi' simply means 'the Church of St David'. 'Brefi', however, is more of a mystery. It can translate as 'bellowing', and one story tells of an ox, killed by the effort of hauling the church stone up a steep hill. Its surviving companion bellowed nine times, and a level track is said to have appeared in the hill. A more straightforward explanation is that 'brefi' refers to the roaring of the nearby brook.

Across the River Teifi lies the site of a Roman fort, where various remains have been found, including a legionary stone bearing a Latin inscription, now set in the wall of a cottage garden.

Llandeilo and Dynevor (Dinefwr) Castle

Map Ref: 86SN6222

The 5th-century saint Teilo gave his name to this town high above the

River Tywi. Until the end of the 19th century, this was the county town of Carmarthenshire; it dates back 700 years, and was once an industrial centre with tanneries, corn and woollen mills.

St Teilo Church, standing beside a 15th-century tower, was rebuilt in the 19th century, but evidence of its past history is seen in its two Celtic cross-heads, made of stone and dating back to the 10th century. Further up the winding street is the imposing Civic Hall, a Victorian building much in use as a community centre, and at the top of Crescent Road, where it is situated, there are splendid views over the Tywi Valley.

On the outskirts of the town is Dynevor Castle, originally a 9th-century fortification, and the possession of the rulers of Deheubarth (south), who squabbled over it for a considerable time. After being subjected to the usual tug-of-war between the Welsh and the Normans, the castle was occupied by the Lord Rhys during the reign of Henry II. By the 18th century, the title of Lord Dinefwr had been inherited through

Gelli Aur Country Park with its arboretum and deer; and two miles further on are the remains of Dryslwyn Castle, 250ft above the Tywi Valley. Although this castle's ruins are confined to a part of the walls and some of the chapel, the surroundings are pleasant, with car parking and a picnic site.

AA recommends:
Hotel: Cawdor Arms, 3-star, *tel.* (0558) 823500
Guesthouse: Llwyndewl Farm Guesthouse, *tel.* (0269) 850362
Self Catering: The Maerdy Cottages, Taliaris, for bookings Mrs M E Jones, Dan-y-Cefn, Manordeilo, Llandeilo, Dyfed SA19 7BD, *tel.* (0550) 777448 or (0328) 51155

Llandovery (Llanymddyfri)

Map Ref: 87SN7634

The old market town which was granted a Charter by Richard III is now a busy little junction – not only for the A4069, A40 and A483, but also for the three rivers, the Brân, Gwydderig and the Tywi.

The town's name can be translated as 'church amid the waters'; it is said that one cannot leave the town from the solid towered Church of St Dingat without crossing water. The statement appears to be true, for passage is impeded to the east by the Brân, to the north-west by the Tywi, and to the north by the Bawddwr, trickling under Cilycwm and Llanfair Road. This stream once flowed down the middle of the street and carried the locals' rubbish and sewage – hence its name, which means 'dirty water'.

The town history dates back to the Romans who, having discovered gold at nearby Pumsaint, built a 5-acre fort to defend the river from anyone trying to gain access to the mines. The insubstantial ruins in the main car park are not Roman, but

marriage by George Rhys (or Rice, for the name had become anglicised), in whose family it remained until fairly recently. Now owned by the West Wales Naturalist Trust, the castle is set in beautiful parkland, laid out by Capability Brown.

Llandeilo is now the administrative centre of the Dynevor region, but has served the Tywi Valley for many years, its markets busy with the local dairy herds, which are considered to be some of the best in Wales.

Three miles west of the town is

those of a Norman castle, the first wooden structure having been replaced by a stone fortification in the 13th century. The castle has all but vanished, but Llandovery's past connection with livestock has not. Its status as an important market town has been retained for centuries, since the days when the drovers herded up their cattle for the long walk to England – and when even pigs, geese and turkeys were driven. This process involved not only stamina but a head for finance, the money for the sales being the responsibility of many drovers. In 1799, Llandovery's Black Ox Bank – one of the first in Wales – was established by David Jones. This bank now carries the symbol of a black horse, and bears another Welsh name: Lloyds.

Alongside the River Brân stands Llanfair-ar-y-Bryn, a church built partly from stonework from the Roman fort. Its graveyard is the burial place of the great hymn writer William Williams, once curate of Llanwrtyd-Wells, until his Methodism prevented his ordination.

The town is also the home of one of the Principality's few public schools, Llandovery College, founded by Dr Thomas Philips in 1848. His intention that scholars should receive tuition through their native language was only fulfilled for a short period, although the college still flourishes and Welsh is still part of the curriculum.

Llandovery's smaller neighbour, Cynghordy, is the site of an impressive 18-arch viaduct which towers above it, carrying the scenic Heart of Wales railway line.

AA recommends:
Guesthouse: Llwyncelyn, *tel.* (0530) 20566
Garage: Newman, New Rd, *tel.* (20836) 21192

Cynghordy lies in a viaduct's shadow

*Evidence of Llandrindod Wells'
Victorian heyday is all around*

Llandrindod Wells

Map Ref: 88SO0561

No one looking at the buildings in
Llandrindod Wells can doubt their
Victorian and Edwardian origins.
Less than 200 years ago, this area
consisted of little more than three
or four farmhouses, an inn,
Caebach Chapel, built in 1715, and
a 'one off' hotel built in 1749
which was later turned into a
woollen mill.

The 19th-century passion for
'taking the waters', combined with
the arrival of the railway in 1865,
resulted in a sudden spate of
building. Even as the war began in
1939, the town's popularity still
centred around the waters, with tea
dances continuing in the Spa
Pavilion and a Palm Court Trio
playing in the mornings.

Although few of today's many
visitors miss the opportunity of
sampling a glass of the famous
waters, they are mainly attracted by
the beautiful scenery and fresh air,
and outdoor activities like golfing,
fishing and bowling tournaments.
But the town has managed to
preserve much of its dignified past,
including the Pump Room, rescued
from a very perilous state about five
years ago, and restored to some of
its former glory with the original
marble counter and mosaic floor.
Other notable buildings are the
Grand Pavilion and a lovely little
19th-century theatre, The Albert
Hall, which produces Old Tyme
Music Hall shows and is the venue
for an annual Drama Festival in
May.

The town's earlier name was
'Ffynnon-llwyn-y-gog' (the Well in
the Cuckoo's Grove), and
indications of the area's earlier life
are all round it, including the 13th-
century St Michael's Church at

Cefnllys, two miles away, standing
above the River Ithon. About 1½
miles north of the town lie the
grassy mounds which were once the
Roman fort at Castellcollen, built in
AD78.

No mention of Llandrindod
Wells would be complete without a
reference to its award-winning
Victorian Festival, which has been
an annual event at the end of the
summer since 1982. For nine days
this compact little town undergoes a
complete transformation, dressing
its shop windows with 19th-century
items, barring cars from the main
shopping street in favour of
carriages and a horse bus, and
expecting everyone to go about
their business in full Victorian dress.
During the last weekend colourful
little street organs stand in twos and
threes on the street corners,
churning out music in turns.

AA recommends:
Hotel: Hotel Metropole, 3-star, tel.
(0597) 2881
Guesthouses: Bailey Einon, tel. (0597)
2449
Brynhir, tel. (0597) 2425
Corven Hall Country, tel. (0597) 3368
Griffin Lodge Hotel, tel. (0597) 2432
Holly, tel. (0597) 2402
Three Wells, tel. (0597) 2484
Campsite: Dalmore Camping Site,
1-pennant, tel. (0597) 2483

Travellers in Wales

The first traveller through
Wales who recorded his
experiences was a medieval
cleric known variously as Gerald of
Wales, Giraldus Cambrensis or
Gerallt Cymro. Through his
writings, Gerald, an astute observer
of people and places, paints a vivid
picture of life in medieval Wales
under the Normans. His books *The
Journey Through Wales* and *A
Description of Wales* were written
in the late 12th century, the former
based directly on his mission to
enlist Welsh troops for the
Crusades. His journey led him
through Hay-on-Wye, where 'the
womenfolk struggle with their men
to stop them volunteering for the
Crusades'.

Gerald was Archdeacon of Brecon,
so by the time he reached Llanddew,
just north-east of the town, he was in
familiar territory. This hamlet, with
its ancient church, was the location of
his 'little house and dwelling . . . I
much prefer it to all the riches of
Croesus, and value it above all the
transitory things of this world'.
Further into central Wales he en-
countered a native nobleman 'ador-
ned by nature, not by art, having a
natural, not an artificial dignity'.

Gerald's enthusiasm for the
Welsh countryside was not shared
by Daniel Defoe, author of
Robinson Crusoe, who, in 1724,
found the Brecon Beacons 'horrid
and frightful, even worse than the

mountains abroad'. William
Wordsworth (1770-1850), the
romantic poet, was not
disappointed by Devil's Bridge. He
visited the falls here in 1824, and
was moved to write a visionary
sonnet to this 'dread chasm'.

George Borrow was also
impressed by Devil's Bridge, a place
he described in uncompromising
terms as 'one of the most
remarkable locations in the world'.
Borrow wrote a classic mid-19th
century travel book, *Wild Wales*
(still in print). The book's title
captures the spirit of Wales's
wildernesses, which have changed
little, in the central heartlands at
least, since Borrow's time. At
Ponterwyd, there is a roadside inn
renamed in honour of the writer,
who sought refuge here from a
particularly exposed and boggy
stretch of the hostile Plynlimon
moorlands. The terrain did not get
any better further south, for he

found 'some of the wildest
solitudes' near Tregaron (anyone
who has driven over the daunting
but exhilarating Abergwesyn Pass
will know what he means) before
arriving in Llandovery, a welcome
sight and 'the pleasantest little town
in which I have halted in the course
of my wanderings'.

Near Llandovery there is an
unusual monument to the age of
stagecoach travel — and Britain's
earliest warning of the dangers of
drinking and driving. On the A40
near the hamlet of Halfway, an
obelisk known as the 'Coachman's
Cautionary' marks the point where
a stagecoach plunged over the side
of the road in 1835. According to
the inscription, the driver, Edward
Jenkins, 'was intoxicated at the
time', so the monument 'was
erected as a caution to mail coach
drivers to keep from intoxication'.

Fourteenth-century travellers

Garages: Automobile Palace, Temple St, *tel.* (0597) 2214
Frank Bright Vehicle Repairs, *tel.* (054781) 200

Llanfihangel Crucorney

Map Ref: 89SO3220

The tiny and ancient village of Llanfihangel Crucorney, now bypassed, was once the site of much activity, when horse-drawn trams came up from Govilon in the early 19th century, bringing essentials like coal and lime, and returning laden with local produce, including apples and cider, corn and hay.

The 12th-century Skirrid Inn, said to be the oldest in Wales, was once the scene of executions, which took place over the stair well during Judge Jeffrey's visit after the Monmouth rebellion.

On certain afternoons in the spring and summer, the 14th- and 16th-century Llanfihangel Court can be explored. This fine stone fronted house boasts four gables and a superb staircase, Jacobean plaster ceilings and much oak panelling, while, outside, there are 17th-century brick stables and pleasant gardens.

Llangammarch Wells

Map Ref: 87SN9347

This pleasant, wooded village, once famous for its medicinal water, sits beneath the Eppynt mountain range, which rises to over 1,500ft, and is surrounded by beautiful countryside.

In previous centuries, the village has had interesting religious connections, and was the birthplace in 1559 of John Penry, 'the Morning Star of the Welsh Reformation'. Born in nearby Cefn Brith farmhouse, he turned from his family's Roman Catholicism to become a zealous Puritan, naming his four daughters Comfort, Deliverance, Safety and Sure Hope, but making many enemies among the English Church and State. His ideas on reformation resulted in his imprisonment and, eventually, execution at the age of 34.

The Skirrid Inn at Llanfihangel Crucorney (above) claims a long and gruesome past. Peaceful countryside surrounds Llangammarch Wells (left)

Llangammarch Wells is today much frequented by anglers, the River Irfon being renowned for its good trout fishing, and the wildlife of the heights can either be enjoyed on foot or from horseback; there is a pony trekking centre nearby.

AA recommends:
Hotel: Lake, 3-star, *tel.* (05912) 202

Llangattock

Map Ref: 92SO2117

Llangattock takes its name from the Celtic saint, Cattwg, who lived in St David's time during the 6th century. Wandering the narrow streets of the village, one can still see attractive cottages built in the days when there was a thriving community of weavers, and when limestone was quarried in the neighbouring hills and transported to the kilns at the wharf on the canal.

Still with its early English tower, the church, first built in the 11th century and restored in 1885, has retained many of its older features, some dating back to the 12th century. As well as an interesting priest's door below the porch, there is a reminder of the fate of miscreants in times past, for inside this beautiful little building the parish stocks and whipping post are kept.

Llangorse Lake (Llyn Syfaddan)

Map Ref: 88SO1326

Over a mile long and half a mile wide, this stretch of water is the largest natural lake in South Wales. Its attractions include sailing, canoeing, rowing, water ski-ing and windsurfing, for all of which a permit is obtainable at the lakeside. The abundant wildlife and interesting plants are suffering, however, from the lake's popularity as a water sport centre, and this causes conservationists no little concern.

A little way from the north-west shore is the man-made island, or crannog, known as Bwlch, built from a huge heap of stones and thought to have held a limited number of dwellings during the Iron Age period. A dug-out canoe of a later period – AD800 – was recovered nearby in 1925, and this can be seen in the Brecknock Museum at nearby Brecon.

The lake, as might be expected, is not without its legends. One tells of a once-thriving township which, destroyed by an earthquake, now lies beneath the lake; the tolling of church bells is said to be heard when the water is rough, and from its tower the Old Woman of Llangorse reaches out to take disobedient children back with her under the water!

Giraldus Cambrensis visited the lake in the 12th century, and claims that the birds here sang only to the true ruler of the Principality. He was certain that the water was 'celebrated for its miracles' being sometimes of 'greenish hue' and then appearing to be 'tinged with red, not universally but as if blood flowed through certain veins and small channels.'

Alas for miracles, it appears that this is only due to the River Llyfni having run over the deep red sandstone, leaving a trail of discolouration until it merges with the lake, the water of which would have been much clearer in the 12th century. It is, unfortunately, a rather mundane explanation for such a mysterious sight.

AA recommends:
Hotel: Red Lion, I-star, *tel.* (087484) 238
Self Catering: The Old Stables, Trefinon Farm (cottage), *tel.* (087484) 607
Campsite: Lakeside Caravan Park, 3-pennant, *tel.* (087484) 226

Llanthony Priory

Map Ref: 89SO2827

Now more commonly known as Llanthony Valley, the Vale of Ewyas is an area of peaceful beauty,

Superb scenery surrounds Llangasty church (top), on Llangorse Lake, and Llanthony Priory (above)

situated along the River Honddu (or Hodni) near the Hereford and Gwent borders of the Brecon Beacons National Park.

The land originally belonged to the Lord of Ewyas in the 12th century, and it was one of his retainers, William de Lacy, who came across the remains of a 6th-century hermitage dedicated to St David. This was Llanthony – a corruption of 'Llan-Ddewi-Nant-Honddu', meaning the 'Church of St David on the River Honddu – and de Lacy decided to stay there, repairing the cell and adopting it as a retreat. By 1108 a church had been consecrated, and the Priory was completed by 1120.

An uprising of the Welsh in 1135 brought the Priory to a state of siege, and a new Priory, Llanthony Secunda, on the banks of the River

Severn in Gloucester, took in nearly all the original inhabitants.

In 1175, Hugh de Lacy provided funds for a new church, the ruins of which are to be seen today, with architecture ranging from Norman to Early English.

By the end of the 18th century, Llanthony had fallen into the hands of Colonel Mark Wood of Brecon, who turned one of its towers into a shooting box; and by the time it was bought by the poet Walter Savage Landor in 1807, it was falling into ruins. The poet's plans, which included planting nearly 10,000 cedars, importing sheep from Spain and building a school, all proved to be impractical.

Fortunately, a great deal of work has been done towards preserving the Priory by the Welsh Office, and regular care is taken of what is now established as an Ancient Monument. Part of the original building is now a bar in the Abbey Hotel, and the 13th-century St David's Church can still be seen.

Llanvihangel
see Llanfihangel Crucorney

Llanwrtyd-Wells

Map Ref: 87SN8746

The sulphur well which brought fame to this, the smallest town in Britain, is still much in evidence by sight and smell alongside the River Irfon, but Llanwrtyd-Wells is worth visiting as more than a historical curiosity. Surrounded by hills of over 1,500ft and beautiful scenery, Llanwrtyd is a truly Welsh town; despite outside influences, over one third of the inhabitants were Welsh-speaking as recently as 1981, and many non-natives are making an effort to learn the language.

The ancient church of St David, around which Pont-rhyd-y-Fferau, the original village, once stood, contains a Celtic cross, a statue of St David and a picture of William Williams, the 18th-century hymn writer and curate of Llanwrtyd.

The influx of visitors to the medicinal springs in the 19th century found Llanwrtyd-Wells only half prepared. Some houses still had clay walls and roofs made of straw and rushes, while the bridge was originally a very dubious wooden structure, continuously repaired until, in 1853, it was replaced by a stone one.

Northwards, along the A483, is the Cambrian Factory, a woollen mill established at the end of World War I to give employment to the disabled. Here the process of manufacturing Welsh tweed can be followed and the products bought.

Llanwrtyd has hosted a wealth of annual activities over recent years, including the Man versus Horse Marathon, an International Four Day Walk, a Beer Festival and a Bog Snorkling Competition – the latter, one suspects, being more enjoyable to watch than to enter!

AA recommends:
Guesthouses: Carlton Court Hotel, *tel.* (05913) 248
Lasswade House, *tel.* (05913) 515
Self Catering: Cwmirfon Lodge Cottages, *tel.* (05913) 217
Kite I & II, Nant Gerreg and Raven Barn, *tel.* (05913) 229

A boater's delight: Llangorse Lake

Llowes *see* Clyro

Llyn Brianne Dam and Reservoir

Map Ref: 87SN7948

This 300ft-high dam, said to be the largest rock-filled dam in Europe, is capable of holding back 13,400 million gallons of water in its 520-acre reservoir. Situated in some of the wildest country in Mid Wales, it can be approached by the scenic steep road from the Abergwesyn to Tregaron pass, or by turning northwards from the A483 towards Rhandirmwyn. Either route then follows the narrow road which skirts the eastern side of the lake.

The site for a new dam to satisfy Swansea's growing demands for water was a matter of controversy in the 1960s, when the original plans to build it at Cwm Senni were overturned by a local campaign. It was thus constructed at Llyn Brianne, on the upper reaches of the River Tywi, where only two farms were submerged. Most of the 20 or so farms which existed on the old valley road in the mid-19th century have, nevertheless, disappeared, and only one, Dolgoch, is now in permanent occupation.

Before the existence of the dam, which took four years to build, access to this remote and beautiful area was difficult; but the necessity of carrying materials to the site brought new, well-surfaced roads, enabling many more people to enjoy this magnificent scenery. The centre of the lake is the meeting point for the boundaries of the old Welsh counties of Breconshire, Cardiganshire and Carmarthenshire.

Some of the supplies from the reservoir now reach Cardiff, and when the water level drops below the spillway, a great mass of spray can be seen shooting out at the bottom, ensuring that adequate provision is continuously made from the river below. There is parking and picnicking space available by the dam, but no fishing or boating is allowed, due to the area's high conservation priority.

Llyn y Fan Fach and Fawr Lakes

Map Ref: 87SN8021

Llyn y Fan Fach, the smaller of these two isolated lakes, and now a reservoir, is approached by road only as far as Llanddeusant, from which it is a walk of some four miles to the east.

The great rock faces and high ridge under which it rests add to the mystical atmosphere of this lovely lake, the setting for an age-old legend. This tells of an enchanting woman who emerged from the lake to marry a farmer's son, with the warning that, should he strike her three times, she would return to the lake with all their possessions. The husband forgot the warning and, so the story goes, was drowned while trying to find his lady of the lake. For years locals are said to have gathered at the lake on the first Sunday in August, believing that she would reappear. After standing beside its dark waters for a while, one would be quite prepared to believe it.

The lake's larger neighbour, Llyn y Fan Fawr, is even more remote and equally haunting, and is reached by climbing to the high ridge above and heading eastwards to Fan Brycheiniog.

Llyn y Fan Fach and Llyn y Fan Fawr mean, respectively, 'small and large lake on the peak'; but anyone who has visited them will agree that the sound of their Welsh names is a far better echo of their splendid isolation amid the mountains.

Maen Llia and Fforest Fawr

Map Ref: 91SN9219

Maen Llia (Llia's Stone) can be an awesome sight, suddenly appearing out of the mists across the remote Fforest Fawr. Its unexpected, eerie presence may account for the strange story that this huge standing stone disappears at cockcrow, when it is said to go down to the river.

Considered to be the best example of a standing stone in the Brecon Beacons National Park, it is at least 12ft high, 9ft across at its widest point and nearly 3ft thick. Its impressive situation at the top of the Llia Valley, over which it points directly north to south, is thought by many to have some spiritual significance. Other studies have produced the less exciting theory that it was used as a landmark, from which travellers took their bearings. Whatever its purpose, there is a mystical aura about this and the other stones erected by the Beaker Folk, about 4,000 years ago.

Fforest Fawr, a vast and often

The picturesque village of Myddfai (right) has produced generations of healers. Victoriana at its best (opposite): New Radnor's memorial to Sir George Cornewall Lewis

lonely area with mountains rising to 1,500ft, was originally a 'Great Forest' – referring to its use as Royal hunting land, rather than the term's present meaning as a place with many trees. It is crossed by the Sarn Helen Roman Road, on one stretch of which, just west of the mountain road to Ystradfellte, there is another stone, the 9ft high Maen Madoc. Standing in a line directly south of Maen Llia, this stone is impressive on its lone, windswept site, and is far older than its Latin inscription – translated as the 'Stone of Dervacus, son of Justus. He lies here'.

After the 'Great Forest' was enclosed in 1815, a lot of the lower land was sold, and sheep farming developed on a large scale. So while the heights can be inhospitable, bleak and misty, with their ancient standing stones and biting winds, the lowlands make a pleasant, pastoral contrast.

Maen Mawr and Cerrig Duon

Map Ref: 86SN8520

Near the source of the Tawe, 1,270ft up, Maen Mawr is a large single stone dwarfing the 1-1½ft high Cerrig Duon stone circle, some 30ft to the south.

Thought to have been erected by the pre-Bronze Age Beaker Folk, possibly as long ago as 2,000BC, the purpose of the stones is uncertain. Ancient shrines and mysterious temples might be intriguing explanations, but the fact that Saith Maen (Welsh for 'Seven Stones'), 3 miles to the south at 1,280ft, are arranged in a line pointing towards Cerrig Duon may confirm the assertion that they are simply route markers.

Only five of the stones at Saith Maen are 'standing', the two largest – one of 9½ft and the other 7½ft – having toppled. The tallest upright stone is 5ft high, but the alignment is still quite clear.

Myddfai

Map Ref: 87SN7730

The little village of Myddfai, at the north of the Black Mountain area, is worth visiting for its interesting

church, with a 14th-century octagonal font and vaulted roof of 15th-century origin. But a more unusual claim to fame is Myddfai's generations of 'healers'. From medieval times to the middle of the 19th century Myddfai's physicians were acknowledged throughout the land – and there are still descendants who claim to have inherited their gifts. Although history and legend are enmeshed, the Myddfai doctors were a fact of life, accompanying the lord of the manor wherever he journeyed. The cures prescribed by Meddygon Myddfai (Physicians of Myddfai) are contained in a medieval manuscript, now housed in the British Museum, revealing a strange mixture of natural medicine, common sense and mystic ideas.

The physicians of Myddfai were said to be descendants of Rhiwallon, thought to have lived around the 12th century and who, legend has it, was taught his powers of healing by his mother, the 'Lady of the Llyn y Fan Fach Lake'.

Mynydd Eppynt (Epynt)

Map Ref: 87SN94

This mountainous terrain, rising to 1,500ft, can be crossed on the B4520, a route giving magnificent views over the hills one minute and plunging into stream-filled valleys the next.

Not far south of Builth Wells, it passes Cwm Owen which, for most of the year is one of the quietest hamlets in the area; if, indeed, 'hamlet' is the correct description for nothing more than a roadside inn. But when the pony sales are held, with horse boxes lining the verges, farmers bidding and dealing, and refreshing themselves with a pint or two of ale, this remote little place suddenly comes to life.

The northern section of the B4520 is very isolated, being mostly moorland and occupied only by sheep. To the west is an artillery firing area; over 50 farms were lost when the army originally took over part of Mynydd Eppynt as a training area during Word War II.

At Upper Chapel, the road is joined by the B4519, once a drovers' track and the only other route to cross Mynydd Eppynt.

New and Old Radnor

Map Ref: 88SO2160, 88SO2559

New Radnor, once the county town until it relinquished the title to Presteigne, now has little to show of its Norman origins other than the site of the hillside castle, built in 1096.

More substantial is the great octagonal memorial to Sir George Cornewall Lewis who, a Londoner by birth, became Member of Parliament for Radnor from 1855 until his death in 1863, during which time he also served as Chancellor of the Exchequer. Often said to be one of the finest examples of a Victorian memorial in the Principality, it is nearly 80ft high, with a base of 25ft in width.

St Mary's Church is also Victorian, having been built in 1845, although there are some 13th-century effigies in the porch. But a much older church is found in Old Radnor, 2 miles to the east. St Stephen's stands on a magnificent hilltop setting, 840ft above sea level on an ancient religious site. This church is such a treasure chest that it is impossible to condense its interesting features, among which is the ancient font, over 1,200 years old and originating as a Druidic altar. Of the Norman church which once existed on the site, only a small piece of a pillar remains, discovered during restoration and now in the vestry; but there are two 13th-century lancet windows in the south wall, a magnificent 15th-century screen and medieval choir stalls, one of which has its old book chain and clasp. The organ case is said to be the oldest in Great Britain, dating from around 1500 and, if some of the Victorian alterations and additions to the furnishings are questionable, the restoration work carried out on the case in 1872 is above reproach.

According to legend, the tolling of the church bells is a signal for the four nearby standing stones, said to be erected over the graves of four warrior kings, to descend to Lake Hindwell for a drink. Anyone choosing to walk up the lane need not follow their course for refreshment; there is an old inn within a stone's throw of the church, along with parking facilities.

Newbridge-on-Wye

Map Ref: 88SO0158

The River Wye runs right past the doorstep of this picturesque valley, accounting for part of its name; the 'new' bridge was built in 1910, to replace the previous wooden structure.

Newbridge church, built in the late 19th century, was founded by a member of the Venables-Llewellyn family, who own Llysdinam Hall overlooking the Wye. Part of their fine grounds now house a Field Study Centre belonging to the University of Wales Institute of Science and Technology, opened in 1970.

Just over a mile away, in the hamlet of Disserth, stands a fascinating little 13th-century church in a delightful setting near the river, with box pews from the 17th century and a pulpit dated 1687. An annual event called the Disserth Wake has recently been revived and involves a fête, music, refreshments and a religious service from the old Prayer Book. During the service everyone crams into the tiny church, packed into the box pews and facing in all directions; and authenticity is lent to the proceedings by the laying of rushes on the church floor.

AA recommends:
Hotel: New Inn, 1-star, *tel.* (059789) 211

Partrishow

Map Ref: 89SO2722

This church serves an isolated community; there is no village, and the building is reached via several narrow lanes, sometimes steep, and eventually climbing to the lych-gate.

Partrishow is thought to have been founded in the 11th century, and the enormous font may well be the original. Its Latin inscription claims that 'Menhir made me in the name of Genillin'; the latter was Prince of Powys before the Norman Conquest.

The original church was called Merthyr Issui after a saint whose cell was near St Mary's stream below the holy well. The approach to the well is indicated by a stone marked with a Maltese Cross, thought to have been a medieval pilgrim's stone.

Mid-15th-century documents record the name of the church as 'Partissw' or 'Partrisw' and, about 100 years later, it appears as 'Partrisso'; how or why the original name disappeared is a mystery.

The church, entered through a 14th-century porch, houses a splendid carved oak screen of the late 15th century, two stone altars in front and a 16th-century 'dug-out' chest made out of one solid tree trunk. Among the interesting wall paintings discovered during restoration in 1909 is one on the west wall of the nave of a 'Doom Figure'; a skeleton with scythe, spade and hour glass. At the west end is a very old double bell-cot with two bells, one of which has an inscription dated 1708.

The locked 13th-century chapel with its altar and six ancient crosses can be visited by arrangement with the Rector in Crickhowell.

The stable building on the lych-gate path contains a reminder that even if the priest of medieval times was spared the difficulty of negotiating the lanes with four wheels, he often got wet; inside is a fireplace which dried his outdoor garments while he was preaching.

Pen y Fan and Corn Du

Map Ref: 88SO0121, 88SO0021

These two mountains are usually mentioned together, being twin peaks of the highest altitude in the Brecon Beacons National Park. Although Pen y Fan's table top

Eisteddfodau

The Royal National Eisteddfod is Wales's most important cultural gathering. This annual festival of music, literature, song and dance, held alternately in the north and south of the country, is the main standard bearer for the traditional, Welsh-speaking face of Wales. But it should not be looked upon in isolation. It stands at the head of a cultural movement which has at its grass roots many modest, local eisteddfodau which take place at towns and villages all over Wales.

The people of Wales – those interested in the survival of its traditional language and culture, at least – cherish the institution of the eisteddfod. But where did it all begin? The first eisteddfod reputedly took place at Christmas in 1176, when the Lord Rhys ap Gruffudd hosted a gathering at Cardigan. In medieval Wales, the skills of the poet – known as the bard – were held in high regard. Bardic competitions were organised, and it was at Carmarthen in the mid-15th century that the term *eisteddfod* (sitting, or session) was first used.

Today's eisteddfod, of course, embraces much more than competitions in poetry, though the chief ceremony at the National Eisteddfod remains the Chairing of the Bard, an honour bestowed on the winning poet. This colourful ritual, presided over by druids cloaked in gold, white, blue and green robes, the Gorsedd of the Bards, is a ceremony that has all the hallmarks of great antiquity. It comes as a surprise to discover that the eisteddfod's bardic rituals are barely 200 years old, the invention of an enigmatic character, part-antiquarian and part-showman, known as Iolo Morgannwg. These rituals first played a part in Welsh eisteddfodau as recently as 1819.

One of the most highly regarded of the local eisteddfodau takes place in the village of Pontrhydfendigaid between Tregaron and Devil's Bridge. Visitors to the village cannot help but notice – and be puzzled by – a huge, oversized barn-like building which looks quite out of place for such a modest little village in the middle of nowhere. It was built there courtesy of the wealthy Sir David James, a local boy made good. Thanks to his patronage, this well-endowed eisteddfod was able to establish for itself a reputation far and wide, which it still enjoys today.

summit is the greatest, at 2,907ft with Corn Du marginally lower at 2,863ft, the difference is not always easily discernible among the Park's soaring heights. Pen y Fan – its name means 'Top of the Peak' – is a favourite with walkers, and on the A470 approach its red coloured track stands out clearly where the sandstone has been exposed – an erosion which the Park authorities are constantly trying to hold in check.

Bronze Age man tended to use the heights as burial grounds, and some of the stone and earth circular mounds are thought to have been made by the Beaker Folk, whose name came from the beaker-shaped vessels buried with their dead.

The monument which stands on the approach to the summit of Corn Du is a reminder of the sad tale of little Tommy Jones, who died in 1900 when he lost his way. No-one will ever know how the

5-year-old managed to climb 1,300ft, for the spot is 2,250ft above sea level; but the obelisk is there for all to see; paid for by a memorial fund to which the jurors at the little boy's inquest gave their fees.

Pontneddfechan
see Porth yr ogof

Pontrhydfendigaid

Map Ref: 87SN7366

This small village with a large name lies near the ruins of Strata Florida,

the 12th-century abbey. The name means 'The bridge near the ford of the Blessed Virgin'.

The village has an enormous hall which was a gift from the late Sir David James and houses a large eisteddfod in May. Hundreds come from miles around to compete in this musical festival. There is genuine 'Welshness' about this event, and it is quite usual to see choirs rehearsing in various corners of the car park or fields – come rain or shine!

Pen y Fan (main picture): the Brecon Beacons Park's highest peak
Inset: the church of Partrishow and (right) its eerie Doom Figure

Pontrhydygroes

Map Ref: 87SN7473

Bordering the River Ystwyth this village, whose name means 'The Bridge near the Ford of the Cross', is situated between Devil's Bridge and Pontrhydfendigaid.

A leading figure in the life of Pontrhydygroes was Thomas Johnes, whose Hafod estate was built up in the 18th century. Although the house was destroyed by fire in 1807, it is immortalised in the book by Elizabeth Inglis Jones called *Peacocks in Paradise*.

Thomas Johnes left his mark in other ways. On the B4574 east of Devil's Bridge is a stone archway, 1,220ft up, which was erected at his instigation to commemorate the golden jubilee of George III.

Pontsticill *see* Taf Fechan

Porth yr ogof and the Waterfall District

Map Ref: 91SN9213

High in the Fforest Fawr (Great Forest) three brooks, Nant Gwair, Nant Mawr and Nant-y-Gaseg, start the River Mellte on its journey southwards. In the limestone area of Ystradfellte the river suddenly disappears underground, into the great, gaping cave of Porth yr ogof. This cavers' delight is a maze of underground passages and caverns, only some of which have been fully explored. It has been established that Porth yr ogof (Gateway to the Cave) has at least 14 entrances besides the most obvious one – which is said to be the biggest in Wales. In spite of its being 16ft high and over 50ft wide, the massive 'gateway' can suddenly become completely flooded, and exploration of the chamber should perhaps be left to the experts.

Having left Porth yr ogof, some ¾ miles to the north, the River Mellte turns into a series of beautiful waterfalls. Sgŵd Clyn-gwyn (Clun Gwyn) is the first, also known as the 'Upper Fall', then comes the Lower Fall, which, with its curved top, is often referred to as a miniature Niagara. Sgŵd y Pannwr (Fall of the Fuller) is the third and smallest, descending to a pool where enormous fish are said to swim, but are impossible to catch.

From nearby Pontneddfechan, near the confluence of the Rivers Mellte, Neath and Sychryd, it is possible to walk downstream to the Mellte waterfalls and Sgŵd Ddwli; and a pleasant route runs north-west to Sgŵd Gwladus, on the River Pyrddin, often known as the 'Lady's Fall'. Gwladus was reputedly one of Brychan, King of Brycheiniog's 26 daughters, living in the 5th century. This fall has a jutting ledge at its summit, but

unlike Sgŵd yr Eira on the Hepste, this does not form a natural bridge behind the cascading water. Beyond the fall is a huge boulder, estimated to be some 17 tons. Unfortunately this has now been overturned, but it was once a Rocking Stone which would move gently back and forth at the touch of a finger.

Among the disused industrial sites near Pontneddfechan are the old silica mines to the east. Part of the train route which once linked them with the Vale of Neath Canal runs under the great 150ft rock Craig y Ddinas.

West of the Pyrddin is Sgŵd Einion Gam, or the 'Crooked Fall', whose change of direction is an impressive sight as it plunges 70ft in a deep ravine.

The famous Sgŵd yr Eira (Fall of Snow), once known as Cilhepste Fall, brings several splendid falls together into one great curtain of foam tumbling off a 3ft overhanging ledge.

The path behind the waterfall is the only way to cross the valley and farmers once drove their sheep over the treacherous route. As well as being very slippery, the path presented some unusual risks. Anyone falling was in danger of being dragged off by a goblin from 'Devil's Glen', as the Hepste Valley was reputed to be full of witches.

The most accessible of the falls in the southern area of the Brecon Beacons is Henrhyd Fall, now in the care of the National Trust. This is a wonderful sight, plunging a sheer 90ft. Any further investigation of the district's falls requires a detailed map; their beauty comes, to a great extent, from their wild and isolated settings.

Presteigne (Llanandras)

Map Ref: 89SO3164

Standing on the River Lugg are the black-and-white timbered houses of Presteigne, which inherited county town status from New Radnor, and later lost it to Llandrindod Wells in the 1974 local government reorganisation.

This was a very lively place in the 18th century, when the busy highway brought a demand for hostelries. Thirty of the buildings

still in existence here were inns, and some of the older ones still serve that purpose, including the Elizabethan Radnorshire Arms, and the Bull. The Duke's Arms is thought to be the oldest, dating from medieval times, with a priest's chamber and, it is said, several secret passages.

A visit to the church of St Andrew's reveals mainly 14th-century features, but there are earlier features: two Norman pillars, and part of the 13th-century tower, from which a nightly curfew is still rung. A 16th-century Flemish tapestry hangs on the wall of the north aisle, and the 1776 carillon, constructed completely in wood and the oldest of its kind in working order, can be visited with the permission of the Rector. Outside, amidst the gravestones, is a memorial stone to 17-year-old Mary Morgan, who was hanged for the murder of her baby in 1805.

Although invaded during the Civil War, the town survived with little damage done, and is one of the places which can truthfully boast that 'Charles I slept here'. The ill-fated King was twice sheltered here, on one occasion at nearby Lower Heath Farm.

Many of Presteigne's buildings were destroyed by the Great Fire in 1681, but fortunately, although the town has lost some of its importance, it has succeeded in retaining all its charm.

The Radnorshire Arms (above), a reminder of the lively past of Presteigne (below). Opposite: two limestone features – a River Mellte waterfall and Porth yr ogof (inset)

Pumsaint

Map Ref: 86SN6540

The five saints referred to in the name of this village are said to have sought refuge under a large boulder – 'Carreg Pumsaint' – which can still be seen nearby. The indentations in the stone are supposed to have been made by their heads and shoulders, but the fact that there are only four impressions spoils the story somewhat, and less fanciful visitors may prefer the theory that it was an anvil base for an ore-crushing mill.

Part of Pumsaint belongs to the 2,600 acres of the National Trust estate, and this is the setting for the Dolaucothi Roman Gold Mines, whose remains stretch above the Cothi Valley for nearly a mile.

The Romans managed to extract about ¾ ton of gold here in only 80 years; probably with the help of expert engineers from northern Spain. Like most Roman projects, the mining involved extensive use of water, which was brought along specially constructed courses – or leats – and released in a flush to wash away the soil and foliage. An ingenious method of retaining valuable particles caught in the flow involved trapping them in gorse branches which were burnt to extract the gold.

Despite several attempts to work the Dolaucothi mines in the 19th and 20th centuries, they finally closed at the end of 1938. Today, the Visitor Centre, opened in 1986, serves as an interesting introduction to this ancient site, where a well marked trail, The Miners' Way, leads to the workings and tunnels. The trail takes over an hour and is fairly steep in parts, making stout shoes a sensible precaution. But there is plenty to see for the less energetic; including a fascinating collection of 1930s mining machinery from a redundant lead mine in North Wales, carefully re-erected to give a complete working atmosphere.

Radnor Forest and Bleddfa

Map Ref: 88SO1964

Originally a forest in the medieval sense – that is, a hunting ground, without necessarily much woodland – Radnor Forest reaches 2,166ft at the highest point of Great Rhos. Over the past few decades, the area has been planted with conifers by the Forestry Commission, and this high ground offers breathtaking scenery.

The road, once an old staging route, was a favourite place for highwaymen, who were said to use

Welsh ponies noting the road signs

A view of the lovely countryside which surrounds Rhayader

stopping off points. One mile north is the old Nant-y-Mwyn Lead Mine, once one of the largest in South Wales, and a flourishing concern by the end of the 18th century. It fell into disuse in 1937, but its present remains include water courses, pits, an engine house and chimney stack. As with most abandoned workings, examination should be carried out with care.

AA recommends:
Guesthouse: Royal Oak, *tel.* (05506) 201
Self Catering: Gelly Farm Cottage, *tel.* (05506) 218
Campsite: Camping and Caravan Club, 3-pennant, *tel.* (05506) 257

Rhayader and Upper Wye Valley (Rhaeadr Gwy)

Map Ref: 88SN9768

Standing on the junction of the A470 and A44, this small market town on the River Wye has a long and turbulent history. In Tudor times, an Assize judge was murdered here by a notorious band of robbers, who raided the town to release one of their number from the gaol. Later, Rhayader was the scene of the Rebecca Riots – a protest against toll gate impositions in the 19th century.

Now a peaceful, picturesque place, Rhayader has a beautiful park, Waun Chapel, laid out by the River Wye, with wooded banks encompassing the old 12th-century castle mound.

The streets radiating from the clock tower, contain cosy old inns, craft shops, pottery and some 17th-century buildings; the tourist office is housed in the Old Swan, which dates from 1683.

A more modern addition is the Welsh Royal Crystal Glass Factory, where visitors are welcome to watch the fascinating art of glass-blowing, and can purchase some of the finished products in the shop. Rhayader fairs date from the days when they were 'hiring' fairs and

Welsh souvenirs at Rhayader's aptly-named Dragon Pottery

there are still pleasure fairs several times a year linked with the livestock markets which take place every Wednesday.

The town's Welsh name means 'The Cataract of the Wye', and although not much of the cataract was left after the bridge was constructed in 1780, there are still small rapids where, in the autumn, one can see the salmon on their way upstream to spawn on the river gravels.

South of Rhayader, the Wye skirts the meadows of the house at Doldowlod, built in the 19th century by the engineer, James Watt, and now the home of Lord David Gibson Watt.

The A470 runs alongside the river as far as Llyswen, but there is a quieter and more attractive route along the B4567 just north of Builth Wells which passes under the great rocks of Aberedw – a favourite area for fossils, and the setting for the cave where Prince Llywelyn is said to have hidden from his enemies.

AA recommends:
Hotel: Elan, West St, 1-star, *tel.* (0597) 810373

the Fforest Inn at Llanfihangel-Nant-Melan as a base. Today, a more likely disruption could well be the sheep which graze the common land, often helping themselves to unsuspecting visitors' picnics!

The northern part of the forest is crossed by the A488, leading to Bleddfa (The Place of the Wolf), where the last wolf in Wales is supposed to have been killed. The village church, standing beside the main road, was fairly recently restored, but the early English font and Jacobean pulpit can still be seen, and from time to time some excellent concerts are given here.

On the opposite corner stands the reputedly haunted Hundred House Inn, dating from the times when the Court of the Hundred was held in Bleddfa, from 1524 to 1867. Those unfortunate enough to be sentenced to death were hanged in front of the 17th-century Monaughty House, still to be seen further along the A488 towards Knighton.

Rhandirmwyn

Map Ref: 87SN7843

This small village is within easy distance of several worthwhile

Twm Siôn Catti

Born out of wedlock in 1503, Thomas Jones, son of Catherine of Tregaron, has become a celebrated figure, part fact, part fiction, and often described as the Welsh equivalent of Robin Hood.

He is believed to have been one of the rebels fighting a Protestant cause against a Catholic government during the reign of Queen Mary. Leaving the country to avoid trouble in about 1557, Twm is known to have reached Geneva, but was back in Wales by 1559 and was eventually granted the return of his lands and a Royal Pardon in 1559. At the age of 77 he married the widow of a Sheriff of Carmarthen ⌐

who lived in Ystradffin – but he died two years later.

The romantic outlaw now associated with Twm Siôn Catti's name was in fact the invention of an 18th-century novelist. The cave near the village of Rhandirmwyn, said to be Twm's hiding place when he was pursued by the authorities, may never have been occupied by the Welsh Robin Hood, but, authentic or not, it attracts plenty of visitors, and the story surrounding it is treated locally with great affection.

The low tunnel which forms the cave's entrance is reached over a river crossing – which should be treated with a fair amount of caution, as the waters here can be very fast-flowing.

Rheidol Power Station and Forest

Map Ref: 86SN7079

The lovely Rheidol Valley is the home of a hydro-electric power station, completed in 1963 and offering an information centre, nature trail and fish farm. On the northern side of the A44 are Dinas and Nant-y-moch, the two reservoirs connected with the hydro-electric system, and popular venues for trout fishing.

Ten miles east of Aberystwyth, the Rheidol Forest has breathtaking views and the Bwlch Nant yr arian Visitor Centre includes exhibitions, slide programmes, a 1½ miles forest trail and a magnificently sited picnic area off the scenic, winding road.

Sennybridge, Defynnog and Llywel

Map Ref: 87SN9228

On the old mail coach road, now the A40, where the River Senni joins the Usk, is Sennybridge – still a busy market town, but now also

the headquarters of the army, who operate on the military ranges over nearby Mynydd Eppynt.

Castell-du (Black Castle) whose ruins lie on the Senni's western bank, earned its name after being used to imprison those who broke the laws of Fforest Fawr. Also on the Senni's banks but further along the main road south, is Defynnog, once a busy agricultural and rural craft centre. Twenty shoemakers are said to have been working here at one time, but over the years Defynnog has lost its importance to Sennybridge, better situated on the east-west highway. Defynnog church, with its 15th-century tower, has an interesting font dated around the 12th century, with an odd inscription thought to be reversed Runic letters; the only one of its kind in Wales.

As the A40 continues westward it passes Llywel, where a cast of the early Christian 'Llywel Stone' is covered in fascinating inscriptions.

First built in the 12th century and called Llantrisant, the nearby church of Three Saints, dedicated to St David, St Padarn and St Teilo, also

A viewing guide on the Sugar Loaf

The South Wales Valleys' water supply: Taf Fechan Reservoir

has a very old font, 15th-century tower and a 16th-century screen, while outside in the churchyard, the village stocks are on display.

AA recommends:

Garage: Sennybridge s/sta, *tel.* (087482) 557

Sugar Loaf Mountain and Ysgyryd (Skirrid) Fawr

Map Ref: 93SO2718

Rising to 1,955ft, north west of Abergavenny, the extinct volcano Sugar Loaf is now in the care of the National Trust and takes its name from the conical top.

The mountain can be explored on horseback along a zig-zag path from Abergavenny, and it is possible to drive a fair way towards the summit by taking the road to Triley.

From the top, a narrow ridge of 300yds or more, a wonderful view stretches right across the Bristol Channel in one direction and over to the Malvern Hills in the other.

Equidistant from Abergavenny but to the north-east, is Skirrid mountain or Ysgyryd Fawr. Its alternative name of the Holy Mountain derives from the story that the ridge developed at the moment of the Crucifixion. On the mountain's 1,595ft summit are the ruins of the medieval Roman Catholic Church of St Michael, once 20ft by 25ft and a shelter for secret Masses during the 17th-century persecution of the Catholics. The surrounding soil, thought to be holy, was scattered on failed crops by local people, who believed it came from the Holy Land or via St Patrick from Ireland.

Taf Fechan Reservoir (Pontsticill)

Map Ref: 92SO0416

This reservoir, completed in 1927, is the last in a chain of four, built to supply water to the growing industrial valley around Merthyr Tydfil. The first, 19th-century reservoir of Pentwyn had been leaking many millions of gallons of water, due to the original dam having been built over a geological fault. This was absorbed into the Taf Fechan, making one large lake, 2½ miles long and holding up to 3,400 million gallons.

In spite of the huge accumulation of water stored above it, the southern regions of the river are in no danger of drying up, some 6.5 million gallons being released from the reservoir daily.

Alongside the reservoir, planted originally by the Water Board and now managed by the Forestry Commission, is a mass of woodland containing coniferous trees. Among the various types of spruce and fir, one can still find the original oak, ash and alder.

A road running along the reservoir's western shore allows visitors to watch the activities of the sailing club, whose slipway is on the opposite side and whose dinghies and windsurfers add a splash of colour to this scenic stretch of water.

Brecon Mountain Railway

In 1980, after eight years of planning, formalities, negotiations and construction, the narrow gauge mountain railway, following part of an old British Rail route, was opened. The train, which is pulled by a vintage steam locomotive, starts its trip at Pant station, 3 miles north of Merthyr Tydfil. Crossing the boundary en route, the journey continues through beautiful scenery as far as the Taf Fechan Reservoir. Passengers can alight here and await the train's return after 20 minutes, or stay to wander through the forest until the last departure in the late afternoon.

The present route covers 2 miles each way, the round trip taking 50 minutes, and there are hopes of extending the line along the eastern side of the reservoir, so that it will eventually run as far as Torpantau Tunnel – 1,313ft above sea level.

For locomotive lovers, a visit to the workshops at Pant Station is a must. Here there are engines built in Germany and the USA as well as examples from Great Britain, including one built by De Winton of Caernarfon in 1894. Some of them have echoes of a far-flung empire; one from Philadelphia was originally ordered by the Eastern Province Cement Company of Port Elizabeth, South Africa. Another, from Hanover, said to be the most powerful steam locomotive built for a 2ft gauge track, worked on the Avontuur Railway and later in Natal, before being brought to the

Brecon Mountain Railway in 1986. A visit in December may be rewarded by an encounter with Father Christmas, who meets the special services run at that time of year.

The original line which ran from Newport to Brecon closed in 1964, after being in existence since the mid-19th century, when it carried iron from industrial South Wales. A remarkable old song tells of 'a guard on Dowlais Branch whose heart was nearly broke; He was working from the morning to the evening of the day, And after he was finished, he was get no extra pay' despite going six and five times back same way. One can only hope the gentleman concerned had plenty of job satisfaction.

A vintage steam engine travels along the Brecon Mountain Railway, against the striking backdrop of Pen y Fan (above)

Talgarth and Bronllys

Map Ref: 88SO1534, 88SO1435

Talgarth, guarded by the impressive heights of Waun Fach and Pen y Gadair Fawr, reveals little of its ancient past today; but there are some interesting features making this small market town worth a visit.

The large church, dedicated to St Gwendoline, dates from the 13th century but was restored in 1873. It is here that Hywel Harris, the father of the Welsh Methodist movement, is buried.

A 13th-century pele tower near the town bridge was once a lookout post, but has now been converted for private dwelling; and although Talgarth's motte and bailey castle, built by the Norman Bernard de Neufmarché in 1088 has not survived, its twin in neighbouring Bronllys can still be seen. This is a rather odd construction, strengthened with stone walls in the 13th century so that its round tower tops the original mound.

Bronllys' Church is of 12th-century origin, but has now been rebuilt. The upper floor of its detached tower was once the hiding place for women and children during times of trouble, while the cattle were sheltered beneath.

Among the area's more modern attractions is a hiring service of horse-drawn caravans, based at Talgarth and supplying tuition if needed.

Strictly for the birds: an 18th-century brick barn with pigeon holes, in Talgarth

AA recommends:
Talgarth
Guesthouse: Upper Genffordd, *tel.* (0874) 711360
Self Catering: Genffordd Farm Cottage, *tel.* (0874) 711360
Campsite: Riverside International Caravan & Camping Park, 4-pennant, *tel.* (0874) 711320
Bronllys
Campsite: Anchorage Caravan Park, 3-pennant, *tel.* (0874) 711246

Talley Abbey

Map Ref: 86SN6332

Founded in the 12th century for the Premonstratensian Order by Rhys ap Gruffudd, Prince of Deheubarth, Talley Abbey was the only house of White Canons in Wales. It was virtually destroyed in the Welsh uprising led by Owain Glyndŵr, and by the time of the Dissolution, there were only eight canons left.

Only ruins remain now of this once magnificent building, originally 300ft long and 100ft high; but even these are a striking sight – especially the north and east walls of the

Founded in 1197, Talley Abbey sits near two lakes, hence its name – a shortened form of Talyllychau, or 'the head of the lakes'

Trecastle, a long street of houses, is a good starting point for mountain walks to Llandovery and Glyntawe

church's central tower, with its two pointed archways.

Talley village or 'Talyllychau' meaning 'the head of the lakes', lies just below these two attractive stretches of water, once used by the Abbey. A public footpath runs alongside the upper lake, but the land surrounding them is privately owned.

Trecastle and Y Pigwn

Map Ref: 87SN8829, 87SN8231

Trecastle, once an old coaching village, still has some of the old buildings and inns which served the travellers in times past. The castle after which it is named is the nearby early 12th-century motte and bailey fortification, the oldest in the Brecon Beacons National Park, and now almost completely covered with beech trees after centuries of neglect.

North-west of the village lies the site of one of the most well known Roman military camps, Y Pigwn, in which a whole legion would stay before moving on to quell local resistance.

Situated on the summit of Mynydd Bach Trecastell, with the Roman road running on its southern side as a link with the great Y Gaer (see page 72), Y Pigwn is now no more than a series of indentations and hummocks – a forlorn ending for such a hive of activity.

AA recommends:
Guesthouse: Castle Hotel, *tel.* (087482) 354

Trefeca

Map Ref: 88SO1432

Trefeca, or 'the home of Rebecca', is named after a house built by a Rebecka Prosser, but is better known as the home of Hywel Harris, the leading figure in the Calvinistic Methodist movement.

Born in 1714, Harris never swerved from his loyalty to the Church of England, but his determination to conduct services, despite not being ordained, incurred the wrath of the Church authorities. After a disagreement with other Methodist Fathers in 1750, Harris set up an early form of commune at Trefeca, encouraging whole families to pool their resources and move in. The project grew to such an extent that a chapel and bath house were built, and farms rented, and before long he had founded the first Agricultural Society in Wales. Sixty trades were carried out at Trefeca, including spinning, weaving, shoemaking, and printing and binding.

From 1842, the house at Trefeca was used as a college for the Methodist Ministry, until 1965, when it became a Non-Sectarian Residential Centre. Many of its original features have now gone but Harris's study is still to be seen, with a circle in the ceiling where there was once a representation of the 'all seeing eye', with 'Jehovah' in black Hebrew characters.

A small Hywel Harris museum is housed in the Memorial Chapel vestry, where there are books printed on the original Trefeca press, linen sheets thought to have been woven there and personal items belonging to Hywel Harris himself, including his pulpit, cruet and candle snuffer.

Tregaron

Map Ref: 87SN6759

Tregaron's association with the surrounding sheep farming community goes back many centuries, and this small market town still has a pleasing atmosphere of the past. Its name, 'Place of Caron', recalls the shepherd boy who became King of Ceredigion in the 3rd century. The church, with its wrought-iron screen and window depicting the *Adoration of the Magi*, is also named after this rags-to-riches figure.

Tregaron's other famous sons include Twm Siôn Catti, the 'Welsh Robin Hood' born at Porth Fynnon House (see page 67); and Henry Richard, founder of the Peace Union (which preceded the League of Nations), who was known as the 'Apostle of Peace'. A statue of Richard stands in the town's central square.

There are several fascinating craft centres here, among which is the Welsh Gold Centre in the Main Square, where goldsmiths work in the old Celtic tradition. At the hand-thrown stoneware pottery in Castell Flemish, 3½ miles to the north, visitors can watch work in progress.

Almost as well known as the town itself is the vast 4-mile area locally known as Cors Caron (Tregaron Bog) or 'Red Bog', because of the colour of the grass in autumn. This is now, in fact, a National Nature Reserve, where sightings of over 160 species of birds have been recorded. However, to explore the reserve a Nature Conservancy Council permit must be obtained.

AA recommends;
Guesthouse: Neuaddlas, *tel.* (09744) 380

Tretower Castle and Court

Map Ref: 88SO1821

In an area strewn with old fortifications one might expect Tretower Castle to be just another ruin. In fact this 11th-century motte and bailey construction is a remarkable sight, with its three-storey tower and 9ft-thick walls giving it a sturdy, menacing aspect. Its links with the nearby manor house, which succeeded it, make it especially interesting.

Built by a Norman called Picard, the castle appears to have been intact as late as the beginning of the 16th century, but its last recorded use was in 1403 when it was fortified against Owain Glyndŵr.

Looking up from the basement it's easy to get an idea of the internal layout, for although the timber roof has been destroyed, the building is substantially intact, and the old living quarters can still be identified.

Standing to the north is the 14th-century fortified manor house of Tretower Court, owned by the Vaughan family for about three centuries. Over the years a great many alterations were made, but many of the original details have survived, including two 14th-century windows and a 15th-century fireplace in the area thought to have been used for Court meetings.

Apart from its examples of architecture, spanning several centuries, the Court is an important illustration of the gradual shift from the medieval castle as a residential headquarters to the domestic building of a more peaceful era.

Usk Reservoir (Cwm Wysg Reservoir)

Map Ref: 87SN8328

The most recent of the reservoirs constructed in the Brecon Beacons National Park is the Usk, completed in 1955 after five years' work.

Set in remote uplands, with Glasfynydd Forest climbing from the shore over the hillside, the reservoir has a capacity of 2,700 million gallons and a dam 109ft high. Walkers can follow the shoreline path around this delightfully peaceful stretch of water, or explore Glasfynydd Forest, in which there are several marked trails.

Fishing is allowed in the 290-acre lake, where there are rainbow and brown trout; permits can be obtained from the Keeper's House.

North of the lake is the Roman camp Y Pigwn and nearby are a number of ancient standing stones.

Y Gaer

Map Ref: 93SO2900

Y Gaer, which simply means 'The Fort', was built by the Romans about AD80, originally of earth and timber; but less than 50 years later it was reconstructed from stone.

Thought to have been in use by the military for just over a century, it was, during its time, a very large and important base. Five hundred Spanish cavalry were housed at the fort, which acted as a focal point for the network of Roman roads, linking forts as far away as Neath,

Remains of a Roman past: Y Gaer, a fort built as the central focus for the soldiers' network of routes, now lies almost forgotten on farmland above the River Usk

Coelbren, Llandovery and Castell-collen.

From the fairly substantial remains, excavated by Sir Mortimer Wheeler, it is possible to make out a more or less rectangular construction, with its walls and gateways clearly visible. These now lie in a peaceful field, which is approached along the A40 from Brecon, taking a minor road north to Aberyscir.

Ystradfellte *see* Porth yr ogof

The Usk Reservoir provides remote beauty – and excellent fishing

Directory

INTRODUCING WELSH

Most people know that the Welsh have their own language, but many visitors are surprised to find that it's very much alive and in evidence all over the country. Welsh is written as it is heard and place-names often include 'mutations' – the softening of a consonant, as in *Gelli*, from the word *celli*.

In pronouncing Welsh words, the stress usually falls on the penultimate syllable. *U* should be pronounced as an *i* or a French *u*; *y* is as *u* in *but* or *i* in *is*; *dd* is as *th* in *the*; and *f* is always pronounced *v*. To achieve the *'ll'* sound, put the side of the tongue against the upper teeth – and blow!

Many road signs are bilingual and the Welsh names can look daunting; but, as this brief glossary shows, they can be an invaluable guide to the history and environment of this fascinating land.

Tackling Welsh place-names can be a daunting prospect, but a noble effort is always appreciated!

Abaty	abbey	Croeso	welcome	Hir	long	Pentre	village
Aber	river mouth	Crib	crest			Plas	hall
Adwy	pass/fate	Cwm	valley	Is	lower	Plwyf	parish
Afon	river	Cymer	junction	Isaf	lowest	Pont	bridge
Allt	wooded eminence/hill	Cymraeg	Welsh	Isel	low	Porth	harbour
Aran	high place	Cymro	Welshman			Pwll	pool
Ardal	district			Llam	leap		
		Dau/dwy	two	Llan	community, church	Rhaeadr (Rhayader)	waterfall
Bach	little	Derwen	oak	Llanerch	glade	Rhiw	ascent
Ban, bannau	peak(s)	Dinas	city	Llech	slate	Rhos	moor
Bechod	pity	Drws	door	Llechwedd	hillside	Rhyd	ford
Bedd	grave	Du (Ddu)	black	Llethr	slope		
Betws	oratory/birch grove	Dwfr or Dŵr	water	Llyn	lake	Saeth	arrow
Blaen, blaenau	head(s) of valley	Dyffryn	valley	Llys	palace/court	Sarn	causeway
Bod	dwelling					Sir	shire
Brenin	king	Eglwys	church	Maen	stone	Sych	dry
Bron	slope	Epynt (Eppynt)	bridle path	Maes	field		
Bryn	hill	Erw	acre	Man	place	Tan	under
Bwlch	gap	Eryri	domain of eagles	Mawr (fawr)	great	Tir	land
Bychan	minor/small	Esgair	long ridge	Melin	mill	Tomen	mound
				Moel	bald/bare hill	Traeth	shore
Cadair (Cader)	chair	Ffordd	road	Môr	sea	Traws	cross
Cae	field	Ffridd	sheepwalk	Morfa	coastal marsh	Tre	town
Caer	fortress	Ffynnon	freshwater well	Mur	wall	Twll	hole
Cafn	trough			Mynydd	mountain	Tŷ, tai	house, houses
Canol	middle	Garth	hill			Tyddyn	smallholding
Cantref	district	Glan	bank	Nant	brook		
Capel	chapel	Glas	blue or green	Neuadd	hall	Uchaf	highest
Cariad	love	Glyn	glen	Newydd	new	Uwch	above
Carn	prominence	Gorsedd	throne	Nos	night		
Carnedd	cairn	Gwaelod	bottom/foot of hill			Y (yr before a vowel, 'r after)	the
Carreg	rock	Gwern	swamp	Ogof	cave	Yn	in
Castell	castle	Gwlad	country	Onnen	ash-tree	Ynys	island
Cefn	ridge	Gwyn	white			Ysbyty	hospice
Celli (Gelli)	grove	Gwynt	wind	Pandy	fulling mill	Ysgol	school/ladder
Clogwyn	precipice			Pant	hollow place	Ysgor	raised defence
Coch (goch)	red	Hafod	summer dwelling	Parc	park	Ystad	estate
Coed	wood	Hendre	permanent winter	Pen	head	Ystrad	river plain
Craig	crag		settlement	Penmaen	rocky headland	Ystum	curve or shape
Croes	cross	Heol	road	Pennant	upper reaches of glen	Ystwyth	winding

ACTIVITIES AND SPORTS

BIRDWATCHING AND BOTANY

Mid Wales has many wildlife sites where you can enjoy nature without harming the environment. Details of nature reserves and conservation are available from the Nature Conservancy Council (see page 79) or from the Wildlife Trust, which has Offices at 8 Severn Square, Newtown, Powys (for Montgomeryshire); Lion House, Brecon (Brecknock); 1 Gwalia Annexe, Ithon Road, Llandrindod Wells, Powys (Radnorshire); and 7 Market Street, Haverfordwest (Dyfed). The following selection lists just a few of the many sites open to visitors.

Castle Woods

The steep slopes of Dynevor (Dinefwr) Castle woods near Llandeilo are home to a wide variety of plant and animal life. Among the scarcer plants is toothwort, a parasite on the roots of the wych elm.

Elan Valley

Thousands of acres of unspoilt upland countryside, easily accessible by road from Rhayader (Rhaeadr). The area has heather, gorse and bracken interspersed with oakwood and pine forests. Buzzard, raven and peregrine are often seen.

Gwenffrwd and Dinas

Ten miles north of Llandovery on the road to Rhandirmwyn. The reserve is owned by the RSPB and covers 1,200 acres. Fine oak woodlands harbour a rich and varied birdlife.

A group of visitors in awe before the largest cave entrance in Wales – Porth yr ogof in Ystradfellte

Tregaron Bog

A reserve managed by the Nature Conservancy Council between Tregaron and Pontrhydfendigaid on the B4343. A prime example of a raised peat bog. Plants include bog mosses, deer grass, bog rosemary and sundews; 40 species of breeding bird have been recorded. Nature trail along old railway line open all year.

The RSPB can give details of birdwatching sites in Mid Wales (see *Useful Addresses*, p79); and the National Trust owns properties rich in wildlife at Abergwesyn Common, Sugar Loaf, Ysgyryd (Skirrid) Fawr, Brecon Beacons, Henryd Falls and Dynevor.

The Forestry Commission has helpful visitor centres at Bwlch Nant-yr-Arian, *tel.* (097085) 694, 10 miles east of Aberystwyth, and at Garwnant, *tel.* (087487) 260, five miles north-west of Merthyr Tydfil.

CANOEING AND BOATING

The rivers and lakes of this area are popular with canoeists and there are numerous activity holiday centres where the sport can be practised.

One of the most scenic canals in Britain passes through the National Park between Brecon and Pontymoile, with six locks and several public houses *en route*. Anyone wanting to use their own boat or canoe should obtain a British Waterways licence from the British Waterways Board Canal Office at Govilon (*tel.* Gilwern 830328). Canoes and rowing boats can be hired for use above Brecon Weir at the Promenade Boathouse; there are also hiring facilities at Llangorse Lake and on the River Wye at Glastonbury. Canoeing on the River Usk is usually restricted to the winter. For information on canoeing events, clubs, training facilities etc contact: The Welsh

Canoe Association, Pen-y-Bont, Corwen, Clwyd LL21 0EL. *Tel.* (0490) 2345

CAVING AND POT-HOLING

The labyrinth of caves under the Brecon Beacons offers some of the longest systems in Britain, though this is not a sport for the ill-prepared or the ill-trained. The four main caving areas in the National Park are in the Tawe Valley, the Ystradfellte area, Nant Glais to the north of Merthyr Tydfil and the Llangattock escarpment above Crickhowell. Ogof Ffynnon Du in the Tawe Valley is so important that it has been designated a National Nature Reserve and rates as one of the longest and deepest caves in Britain, with 28 miles of passage. Two show caves in the Tawe Valley near Craig-y-nos – Dan-yr-Ogof and Cathedral caves – provide 2½ hour guided tours of the show complex. The co-ordinating body for the sport in Wales is The Cambrian Caving Council, Ynys Isaf, Ystradgynlais, Swansea. *Tel.* (0639) 849519

GOLF

Aberystwyth Golf Club, Brynmor, Aberystwyth, Dyfed SY23 2HY. 18-hole course overlooking town and Cardigan Bay. Visitors welcome; must be members of bona fide club. *Tel.* (0970) 615104

Bryn Meadows Golf and Country Club, The Bryn, near Hengoed, Mid Glamorgan CF8 7SM. 18-hole parkland course off A472, Ystrad Mynach to Blackwood. Visitors welcome any time except Sunday mornings. *Tel.* (0495) 225590

Builth Wells Golf Club, Golf Links Road, Builth Wells, Powys LD2 3NF. 18-hole parkland course. Visitors

welcome any time, must be
members of bona fide club. *Tel.*
(0982) 553296

Glynhir Golf Club, Glynhir Road,
Llandybie, Dyfed SA18 2TF.
18-hole parkland course near
Llandyfan. Visitors welcome any
time. *Tel.* (0269) 850472

Morlais Castle Golf Club, Pant,
Merthyr Tydfil, Mid Glamorgan
CF48 2UY.
Nine-hole course 3 miles north of
Merthyr Tydfil. Visitors welcome
any time except Saturdays. *Tel.*
(0685) 722822

Penoyre Park, Cradoc, Brecon,
Powys LD3 9LP.
18-hole course 3 miles north of
Brecon. Visitors: weekdays without
reservation, weekends by
arrangement; must be member of
recognised club. *Tel.* (0874) 3658

Pontypool Golf Club, Trevethin,
Pontypool, Gwent NP4 8DJ.
18-hole hillside course one mile
north-east of Pontypool. Visitors
welcome; must be bona fide golf
members with a handicap. *Tel.*
(04955) 3655

Rhosgoch Golf Club, Builth Wells,
Powys LD2 3JU.
A nine-hole parkland course located
5 miles north of Hay-on-Wye.
Visitors welcome any time

PONY TREKKING
The rambling, uncrowded hills and
vales of Mid Wales are a delight for
riders, and the little town of
Rhayader claims the distinction of
being one of the first ever centres
for this activity.
    The following centres offer
accommodation and tuition as well
as daily or half-day treks. They all
meet the standards set by the Pony
Trekking and Riding Society of
Wales.

Abergavenny
Black Mountain Holidays
The Youth Hostel, Capel-y-ffin,
Abergavenny, Gwent NP7 7NP.
Tel. (0873) 890650
Grange Trekking Centre
The Grange, Capel-y-ffin,
Abergavenny, Gwent NP7 7NP.
Tel. (0873) 890215
Neuadd Farm Pony Trekking Centre
Neuadd Farm, Cwmyoy,
Abergavenny, Gwent NP7 7NS.
Tel. (0873) 890276
Pine Grove Riding Centre
Llanwenarth, Abergavenny, Gwent
NP7 7ET.
Tel. (0873) 810228
Trewysgoed Trekking Centre
Trewysgoed Forest, Abergavenny,
Gwent NP7 7LW. *Tel.* (0873)
890296

Aberystwyth
Moelfryn Riding Centre
Moelfryn Mawr, Bethania,
Aberystwyth, Dyfed SY23 5NA.
Tel. (09746) 228

*Boating can be enjoyed on Llangorse
Lake, the biggest natural lake in South
Wales*

Brecon
Black Mountain Riding Holidays
Pen y Bryn, Llangorse, Brecon,
Powys LD3 7UG.
Tel. (087484) 272
Cadarn Trail Riding Holidays
Velindre, Three Cocks, Brecon,
Powys LD3 0SP. *Tel.* (04974) 680
Cantref Trekking Centre
Brecon, Powys LD3 8LR. *Tel.* (087
486) 223
Trans-Wales Trail Rides
Cwm-fforest RC, near Talgarth,
Brecon, Powys LD3 0EU. *Tel.*
(0874) 711398
Tregoyd Riding Centre
Tregoyd, Three Cocks, Brecon,
Powys LD3 0SP. *Tel.* (04974) 351

Builth Wells
Castle Rhosgoch Trekking Centre
Rhosgoch, Builth Wells, Powys
LD2 3JU. *Tel.* (04975) 242/251
Lower Hall Riding School
Maesmynis, Builth Wells, Powys
LD2 3HP. *Tel.* (0982) 552479
(No accommodation but can be
arranged nearby)

Llandrindod Wells
Range Rides
Blaen-y-Cwm, Llanwrthwl,
Llandrindod Wells, Powys LD1
6NU. *Tel.* (0597) 810627

Merthyr Tydfil
Pengelli Fach Farm and Riding School
Pontsticill, Vaynor, Merthyr Tydfil,
Mid Glamorgan CF48 2TU. *Tel.*
(0685) 2169

Newtown
The Mill Trekking Centre
Llwydcoed Mill, Aberhafesp,
Newtown, Powys SY16 3JE. *Tel.*
(0686) 84440

Rhayader
*The Lion Royal Hotel and Trekking
Centre*
Rhayader, Powys LD6 5AB. *Tel.*
(0597) 810202

Overland Pony Trek
Ddole Farm, Rhayader, Powys LD6
5HG. *Tel.* (0597) 810402
Rhayader Pony Trekking Association
Nantserth House, Rhayader, Powys
LD6 5LT. *Tel.* (0597) 810298

Talgarth
Welsh Horse-Drawn Holidays
Rhydybont, Talgarth, Powys LD3
0EE. *Tel.* (0874) 711346

RESERVOIR FISHING
The Welsh Water Authority owns
many reservoirs in the Mid
Wales/Brecon Beacons area which
are regularly stocked and offer
fishing in season (20 Mar-17 Oct).
Separate permits are required for
angling on these fisheries. 'Rover'
permits are available from The
Estates and Recreation Officer,
Welsh Water, South East Division
HQ, Pentwyn Road, Nelson,
Treharris, Mid Glamorgan
CF46 6LY. *Tel.* (0443) 4505077

Elan Valley Reservoirs
A group of five reservoirs high in
the hills above Rhayader. Fly fishing
only on the reservoirs but spinning
and worming permitted on the
streams. No boats. Details of season
and day permits from Elan Estate
Office, Elan Village, Rhayader. *Tel.*
(0597) 810449

Llandegfedd Reservoir
Near Pontypool, 12m from
Newport. Bank fishing from 7am to
monthly closure times advertised on
site. Fly fishing only. Boats available
for hire (pre-booking advised). *Tel.*
(04955) 55122

Llwyn-On Reservoir
Bordered by a mature conifer forest
in the National Park just off the
A470 Brecon-Merthyr Tydfil road.
150 acres of high quality brown
and rainbow trout fishing waters.
Open from 8am. Day permits
available from machine at new
Llwyn-On water treatment works.
Tel. (0443) 450577 (Welsh Water
Authority)

Beautiful walkers' country at Cwmyoy, in the Vale of Ewyas

Talybont Reservoir
Set in a wooded valley in the National Park 8 miles from Merthyr Tydfil. The largest fish ever taken here weighed over 13lbs. Open from 8am to monthly closure times. Day permits available from machine at nearby water treatment works. Fly fishing only. No fishing from dam face and overflow. *Tel.* (0443) 450577 (Welsh Water Authority)

Upper Neuadd Reservoir
Set in outstanding scenery at the top of the Taf Fechan Valley between Brecon and Merthyr Tydfil on the road to Talybont. Open from 8am to monthly closure times. Managed as a wild brown trout fishery. Fly fishing only; no boats. *Tel.* (0443) 450577 (Welsh Water Authority)

Usk Reservoir
An attractive upland reservoir and one of the best trout fisheries in Wales. Fly fishing, spinning and worming are allowed. Open from 8am to monthly closure times. Anglers are permitted to use their own boats by arrangement only. *Tel.* (087482) 554

ROCK CLIMBING

The opportunities for rock climbers in this area are limited to outcrops of quarried limestone which should always be treated with caution, particularly after rain when they become very slippery.
There are several main crags to be found in the park. Dinas Rock, near Pontneddfechan, has a steep face 120ft high, providing a good standard of climbs; but adjoining it

is an easy angled slab, which is a good training area for novices.
Cefn Coed, near the A465, to the north of Merthyr Tydfil, offers a variety of routes of up to 110ft in height. In the same area is Morlais Quarry on the northern slopes of Morlais Hill. This is undoubtedly the best crag in the National Park. Routes of all standards are listed in the guide book and the rock is of good quality although rather polished, due to its popularity. There are three tiers of cliffs available: Upper, Middle and Lower.
Taf Fechan crag is to the south of Pontsticill, but the rock is unreliable and has never proved a particularly popular cliff for climbing. On the hill above are the Twyniau Gwynion quarries, involving a walk to get there but providing some interesting short climbs of varying standards.
The Llangattock escarpment above Crickhowell also provides climbing on long-abandoned quarry faces. The most popular one is at Chwar Pant y Rhiw, more popularly known as Pinnacle Bay. This crag has been well developed and is in frequent use by the local outdoor activity centres. At the western end of the escarpment is Craig y Castell, which can be reached from the Llangattock to Beaufort road. The routes are steep but more varied than those at Pinnacle Bay.

WALKING

The Park's Mountain Centre just off the A470 at Libanus, south of Brecon, gives advice and information on the many walks available in the Brecon Beacons. Sudden changes in the weather, coupled with inadequate clothing, equipment or knowledge can easily result in misfortune or tragedy. The

summits of the Beacons are nearly 3,000ft high, and it is advisable to check the weather forecast before setting out (*tel.* (0898500) 414). Be prepared to alter or abandon your route if the weather changes for the worse or proves unsuitable for members of your party. Leave details of your route (and stick to it) with a responsible person and report your return to them. Members of a walking party should be equipped with sensible footwear and warm or waterproof clothing. Waterproofs should always be carried, even if the weather is fine when you set off, for it is surprising how quickly conditions can change in the hills. For winter walking, carry or wear gloves, hat and extra warm clothing. In addition, a map, compass, whistle, torch, first aid kit and extra food for emergencies (eg, chocolate) should be kept in the rucksack for every walk. There are several country walks along the Welsh borders, and details can be obtained from the Offa's Dyke Centre, Knighton. *Tel.* (0547) 528192

CRAFT CENTRES

Mid Wales is the most rural area of the Principality and small cottage industries related to the weaving of woollen products are commonplace. But there are other crafts available too – pottery, wood carving, leather, basketry and even candlemaking. Craft workers are generally pleased to welcome visitors, but it is best to ring first, to check on opening times.
Information on other centres in Mid Wales is available from local Tourist Information Centres.

Ammanford
D Thomas & Son Weaving, Cwmllwchwr Woollen Mill,

Ammanford. Near Technical College. Weaving by shuttle and rapier loom can be seen free of charge. Shop. *Tel.* (0269) 2503

Brecon
Glynderi Pottery, Sennybridge, near Brecon. Stoneware pottery for kitchen and garden. *Tel.* (087482) 564
Llyswen Pottery, Llyswen, near Brecon. Traditional slip-decorated and multiglazed earthenware. Shop, refreshments. *Tel.* (087485) 388
Wye Clocks, Pen y Garn, Boughrood, Llyswen. Hand painted wall clocks for kitchens and nurseries; also personalised designs to customers' specifications. *Tel.* (087485) 340

Builth Wells
One and Only Woollies, Corn Mill Craft Shop, Trecricket Mill, Erwood (on A470 1½m from Llyswen). Designer knitwear in wool and fancy yarns. Original designs, craft shop. *Tel.* (09823) 312
Taylors Woolcrafts, Park House, 15 Park Road (on A483 to Llandovery, opposite fire station). Hand knotted wool hearth rugs, hand knit pullovers. Sales room, refreshments, demonstrations. *Tel.* (0982) 552403
Woodgrain Crafts, Erwood Station, Llandeilo Graban, Builth Wells. Woodturning craftsman in converted station. Showroom with other local crafts. Refreshments, picnic area. *Tel.* (09823) 674
Woodwise of Cilmeri, Old School House, Cilmeri, near Builth Wells. High quality hand turned and finished articles – clocks, barometers, goblets, plaques, lamps. *Tel.* (0982) 553572

Crickhowell
Furniture Making and Restoration, Graham Amey Ltd, The Granary, Standard Street, Crickhowell. Individually made furniture for home and contract. Commissioned dressers, wall units, tables. Showrooms and workshop open. *Tel.* (0873) 810540

Newtown
First Flight Jewellery, The Old Sawmill, Tregynon, Newtown (5m north of Newtown on B43/B4389 to Llanfair Caereinion). Ornamental gemtrees using semi-precious stones. Jewellery, badges, clocks. Refreshments. *Tel.* (068687) 544

Rhayader
Welsh Royal Crystal Glass Factory, Bryn Derth Industrial Estate, Rhayader. Guided tours of the glass-making factory, Mon-Fri 11am and 11.20am; 2pm and 2.20pm. Shop (Mon-Fri 10am-5.30pm, weekends 10am-5pm). *Tel.* (0597) 811005

Skenfrith, Nr Abergavenny
Studio Dyed Yarns, Hope Garden, Skenfrith (on B4521 Abergavenny –

Information in an industrial setting at the Blaenavon Big Pit Mining Museum

Ross on Wye). Studio-dyed skeins, knitting/rug kits, high quality knitted garments, commissions accepted. Shop. Spinning and weaving demonstrated. *Tel.* (060084) 607

Tregaron
Craft Design Centre, Main Square, Tregaron. Celtic traditional jewellery, knitwear in natural homespun Welsh wools. Licensed users of Welsh gold. Shop. *Tel.* (09744) 415
Stoneware Pottery, Castell Flemish, Tregaron (3m north of the town on the A485 Aberystwyth road). Hand thrown and decorated stoneware pottery. Workshop and shop open to visitors. *Tel.* (097421) 639

INFORMATION CENTRES

Full tourist information is available from the centres detailed in the following list. See also the *Directory* entry *Useful Addresses.*

Open All Year:

Aberystwyth
Ceredigion District Council, Eastgate. *Tel.* (0970) 612125/611955

Knighton
Offa's Dyke Association, The Old School. *Tel.* (0547) 528753/528529

Llandrindod Wells
Rock Park Spa. *Tel.* (0597) 2600

Llanwrtyd-Wells
The Bookshop. *Tel.* (0591) 3391

Machynlleth
Canolfan Owain Glyndŵr, Maengwyn Street. *Tel.* (0654) 2401

Monmouth
Church Street. *Tel.* (0600) 3899

Newport
Newport Museum Centre, John Frost Square. *Tel.* (0633) 842962

Tredegar
Bryn Bach Country Park. *Tel.* (0495) 711816

Open Summer Only:

Abergavenny
2 Lower Monk Street. *Tel.* (0873) 3254/77588

Blaenavon
Big Pit Mining Museum. *Tel.* (0495) 790122

Brecon
Market Car Park. *Tel.* (0874) 2485/5692

Builth Wells
Groe Car Park. *Tel.* (0982) 553307

Elan Valley
Elan Valley Visitor Centre. *Tel.* (0597) 810898

Llandovery
Central Car Park, Broad Street. *Tel.* (0550) 20693

Llanidloes
High Street. *Tel.* (05512) 2605

Merthyr Tydfil
14a Glebeland Street. *Tel.* (0655) 79884

Tintern
Tintern Abbey. *Tel.* (02981) 431

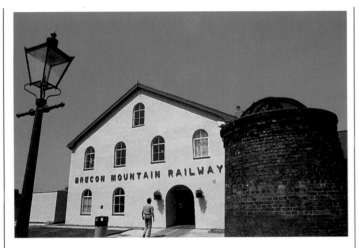

The Brecon Mountain Railway: a pleasant way to reach the Beacons

PLACES TO VISIT

CASTLES AND HISTORIC SITES

The borderlands of Mid Wales have a turbulent past. The Romans were garrisoned here to keep the Welsh in check; then came the Normans, and later the Wars of the Roses. Today, evidence of these violent times can still be seen in the many castles and forts worth visiting.

Religion flourished as well as war, and the abbeys and churches of Mid Wales and the border country still retain an atmosphere of peace and tranquillity.

Listed here are some of the major historic sites. Many are now in the care of Cadw: Welsh Historic Monuments, who operate the following standard opening times: 15 Mar-15 Oct, weekdays 9.30am to 6.30pm; Sun 2pm to 6.30pm. 16 Oct-14 Mar, weekdays 9.30am to 4pm; Sun 2pm to 4pm.

Abbeycwmhir *Near Llandrindod and Rhayader.*
Some traces of outside walls, bases of several nave piers and fragments of transepts are all that remain of this abbey, thought to have been founded in the 12th century. But the tranquil setting in the hills above Llandrindod makes it well worth a visit. Open at all times.

Abergavenny Castle.
Only fragments remain of this castle, which once belonged to the notorious William de Braose, whose name became a by-word for treachery and cruelty in the Welsh Marches. Open at all times.

Carreg Cennen Castle (Cadw) *Near Llandeilo.*
Sited on a limestone crag nearly 300ft above the scenic Tywi Valley, this castle has a lively history. A fascinating feature is a vaulted passage leading to a cave deep beneath the castle, and the Rare Breeds Centre is an added and contrasting attraction. See standard opening times.

Castell-y-Bere *Abergynolwyn.*
Dramatically sited in the shadow of Cadair (Cader) Idris, this Welsh castle is now a lofty ruin. A lonely mountain stronghold, it was captured by Edward I. Open at all times.

Dolaucothi Roman Gold Mines (NT).
These open cast mines, now in the care of the National Trust, honeycomb the hills above Pumsaint in Dyfed. Guided tours below ground (daily, Jun-Sep) and a visitor centre with explanatory displays (daily Etr-end Oct). *Tel.* (05585) 359

Llanthony Priory.
Set on the River Honddu in the Vale of Ewyas, this majestic ruin still has a 13th-century church; a bar has been built into the original building. See standard opening times.

Montgomery Castle.
Perched high on a rock, these ruins command a fine view of the borderland town. The castle dates from 1223 and was built by Henry III but destroyed by the Roundheads in 1649. Open at all times.

Strata Florida Abbey (Cadw).
Set in the remote hills near the village of Pontrhydfendigaid (Dyfed), this lovely ruin has a magnificent archway and floor tiles. Also here is a memorial slab to Dafydd ap Gwilym, the 14th-century Welsh lyric poet who is believed to be buried under a yew tree in the grounds. See standard opening times.

Talley Abbey (Cadw) *North of Llandeilo.*
Although much of this 12th-century abbey has been swept away, the central tower of the church survives almost to its full height, overlooking the remains of the nave. A beautiful setting in the hills at the head of the Talley lakes. See standard opening times.

Tretower Court (Cadw) *Crickhowell.*
A stately home dating from the late Middle Ages; its ancient walls and spacious rooms give a flavour of life in those days. This was the home of the Vaughan family – including the metaphysical poet Henry Vaughan. Individual 'Soundalive' cassette tours. See standard opening times. *Tel.* (0874) 730279

White Castle (Cadw) *Abergavenny.*
With nearby Skenfrith and Grosmont, White Castle formed a defensive triangle in the days when the Marcher lords were troubled by the unruly Welsh. Substantial ruins. See standard opening times.

Y Gaer Roman Fort *Brecon.*
Y Gaer (the Roman name was probably *Cicutium*) was a large inland fort manned by auxiliaries, founded about AD80. Remains of the south gateway stand 8ft high in places. Excavations have revealed the layout of the buildings and granary. Open at all times.

MUSEUMS AND OUTDOOR ATTRACTIONS

Brecon
Brecknock Museum
This museum centres around a tiny assize court which remains intact with bench, prisoner's dock, etc. The traditional rural life of the region is illustrated by means of displays of farm implements and a superb collection of Welsh love spoons. Complete smithy open to visitors. Open Mon-Sat, all year from 10am to 5pm. *Tel.* (0874) 4121

Brecon Mountain Railway *Pant, near Merthyr Tydfil.*
A narrow-gauge railway which follows a 2-mile route from Pant into the foothills of the Brecon Beacons. Attractive walks from lakeside halt at Pontsticill. Café, shop. Open May-Sep, Tue, Wed and Thu, 10.30am to 4pm. *Tel.* (0685) 4854

Dan-yr-Ogof Showcaves *(between Brecon and Swansea on the A4067 at Abercraf).*
A complex of three large showcaves and a Dinosaur Park, this attraction has won seven major tourism awards. Guided tours underground last a minimum of two hours. Dry ski slope and instruction also available to visitors. Self-catering chalets available on site. Restaurant, craft shop, museum and information centre. Open daily Etr – end Oct from 10am. *Tel.* (0639) 730284

Elan Valley Visitor Centre
A 45,000-acre estate in the care of the Welsh Water Authority. It has four dams and is the best inland ornithological site in Wales. Excellent walking, viewpoints and

picnic areas. The new Visitor Centre has exhibition and audio-visual theatre. Access to estate all year round. Visitor Centre open Etr – Oct. *Tel.* (0597) 810880

Garwnant Forest Visitor Centre (*5 miles from Merthyr Tydfil on the A470 towards Brecon*).
Run by the Forestry Commission, this Centre overlooks the Llwyn On Reservoir. A focal point for the forests of the Brecon Beacons. An exhibition and audio-visual programme explains how farming, forestry, and water-supply needs have fashioned the landscape. Open Etr – end Sep (weekends: afternoons only). *Tel.* (087487) 260

Gelli Aur Country Park
Situated 3 miles west of Llandeilo, the park has nature trails and an arboretum, and the deer are fed every afternoon at 2pm. Open daily to end Aug.

Hywel Harris Museum *Trefeca.*
A museum showing books, sheets and personal items belonging to the founder of a Welsh Methodist community. Open Mon-Fri, 10am to 4pm; Sat during summer.

Llandrindod Wells *Rock Park Spa.*
An opportunity to relive the elegance and tranquillity of Victorian times. Play outdoor chess or croquet; take the waters, or have a Welsh tea in the Pump Room. An exhibition in the former Bath House tells the history of the spa town. Set in 18 acres of natural parkland. Open all year daily, admission free. *Tel.* (0597) 4307

Llanwrtyd-Wells *Cambrian Factory.*
Free, unconducted tours with audio-visual introduction of a fully working mill. See the processes of dyeing, blending, carding, spinning and weaving. Open all year (not weekends). *Tel.* (09531) 211

Llywernog *Silver Lead Mine.*
A six-acre 'Pioneer Park' at Ponterwyd, 11 miles east of Aberystwyth. The museum has working water wheels, old mining and agricultural machinery, exhibitions, underground tunnels and more – all linked by a 'Miner's Trail'. Open Etr – Oct. *Tel.* (097085) 620

Vale of Rheidol Narrow Gauge Railway *from Alexandra Road, Aberystwyth.*
This line follows a scenic route to the magnificent waterfalls at Devil's Bridge. Open Etr – Oct, weekdays, 10.15am to 4.15pm; weekends 10.15am to 2pm. *Tel.* (0970) 612377

Wolves Newton *Model Farm Rural Centre.*
This centre near Chepstow includes a Victorian Folk Museum, craft workshops, pure breeds of poultry and waterfowl and farm animals.

Licensed restaurant, picnic area, adventure playground. Open Etr – end Sep daily, 11am to 6pm; Oct and Nov weekends only, 11am to 6pm. *Tel.* (02915) 231

USEFUL ADDRESSES

Details of regional information centres are contained in a separate section within this Directory. Additional information for visitors can be obtained from local tourist board offices and local authorities.

Brecon Beacons National Park Authority,
Watten Mount, Brecon, Powys LD3 7DP (written enquiries only).

Cadw: Welsh Historic Monuments,
Brunel House, 2 Fitzalan Road, Cardiff, South Glamorgan CF2 1UY. *Tel.* (0222) 465511

Countryside Commission,
Wales Office, Ladywell House, Newtown, Powys SY16 1JB. *Tel.* (0686) 26799

Forestry Commission,
Victoria House, Victoria Terrace, Aberystwyth, Dyfed SY23 2DQ. *Tel.* (0970) 612367

National Trust,
South Wales Office, King's Head, Bridge Street, Llandeilo, Dyfed SA19 6BN. *Tel.* (0558) 822000

Nature Conservancy Council,
Plas Gogerddan, Aberystwyth, Dyfed SY23 3EB. *Tel.* (0970) 820295

Offa's Dyke Association,
Old Primary School, West Street, Knighton, Powys LD7 1EW. *Tel.* (0547) 528753

Royal Society for the Protection of Birds,
Bryn Aderyn, The Bank, Newtown, Powys SY16 2AB. *Tel.* (0686) 626678

Sports Council for Wales,
National Sports Centre, Sophia Gardens, Cardiff, South Glamorgan CF1 9SW. *Tel.* (0222) 397571

Wales Tourist Board,
Head Office: Brunel House, 2 Fitzalan Road, South Glamorgan CF2 1UY (written enquiries only). For leaflets and publications: PO Box 1, Cardiff, South Glamorgan CF1 2XN.

Wales Tourist Board,
South Wales Regional Office: Tŷ Croeso, Gloucester Place, Swansea, West Glamorgan SA1 1TY. *Tel.* (0792) 465204

Welsh Water Authority,
The Recreation Section, Cambrian Way, Brecon, Powys LD3 7HP. *Tel.* (0874) 3181

A brain-teasing attraction at Llandrindod Wells is outdoor chess

CALENDAR OF EVENTS

Visitors to the Brecon Beacons and Mid Wales are well-placed to enjoy a wide range of entertainments. The towns of Newport, Cwmbran, Merthyr Tydfil and Builth Wells offer festivals and shows; and in the deep rural areas, the accent is on informality and local talent. For details of events in small towns and villages enquire at the local Tourist Information Centre. A free annual events diary is published by the Wales Tourist Board and is available at all TICs.

March

Newport Drama Festival, The Dolman Theatre, Newport

Annual Welsh Beekeeping Convention and Fair, Royal Welsh Showground, Llanelwedd, Builth Wells

April

Live at Llantrisant, Cross Keys Hotel, Llantrisant (music nights held every Wednesday)

Annual Welsh Antiques Fair, The Castle of Brecon Hotel, Castle Square, Brecon

Pontnewydd Male Choir, Annual Concert, Cwmbran Stadium, Cwmbran

April-May

Llantilio Crossenny Festival of Music and Drama, St Teilo's Church, Llantilio Crossenny, near Abergavenny

Welsh National Open Showjumping, Royal Welsh Showground, Llanelwedd, Builth Wells

May

Twmbarlwm Trek, Risca Leisure Centre, Risca, Gwent (annual cross country challenge walk in the Gwent valleys)

Peterston Wentloog Horse Show and Gymkhana, Tredegar House, Newport

June

June 1-September 30:

Mid Wales Festival of the Countryside, at various venues and locations throughout Mid Wales. More than 500 countryside events with the visitor in mind. Details from TICs

Welsh National Steam and Agricultural Show, Royal Welsh Showground, Builth Wells

Man versus Horse Marathon, The Square, Llanwrtyd-Wells

Aberystwyth Agricultural Show, Tanycastell Park, Rhydfelin, Aberystwyth

July

Abergavenny Summer Festival, various venues

Royal Welsh Show, Llanelwedd Showground, Builth Wells (biggest agricultural show in Wales)

July-August

Aberystwyth Summer Festival, various venues

Royal National Eisteddfod of Wales. 1989: Llanrwst; 1990: Rhymney Valley

September

Usk Agricultural Show, Trostrey Court Farm, Usk

Llandrindod Wells Victorian Festival

October

Swansea Festival. Concerts at Brangwyn Hall and a wealth of fringe events throughout the city

November

Mid Wales Beer Festival, various inns, Llanwrtyd-Wells

December

Christmas Craft Fair, Aberystwyth Arts Centre

Male voice choirs are a well-established part of the Welsh cultural tradition

BRECON BEACONS
AND MID WALES

Atlas

The following pages contain a legend, key map and atlas of Brecon Beacons and Mid Wales, four motor tours and sixteen walks.

Above: Abergwesyn Common – a lonely expanse of open moorland

Legend

GRID REFERENCE SYSTEM

The map references used in this book are based on the Ordnance Survey National Grid, correct to within 1000 Metres They comprise two letters and four figures, and are preceded by the atlas page number.

Thus the reference for BRECON appears 88 SO 0528

88 is the atlas page number

SO identifies the major (100km) grid square concerned (see diag)

0528 locates the lower left-hand corner of the kilometre grid square in which BRECON appears.

Take the first figure of the reference 0, this refers to the numbered grid running along the bottom of the page. Having found this line, the second figure 5 tells you the distance to move in tenths to the right of this line. A vertical line through this point is the first half of the reference.

The third figure 2, refers to the numbered grid lines on the right hand side of the page, finally the fourth figure 8 indicates the distance to move in tenths above this line. A horizontal line drawn through this point to intersect with the first line gives the precise location of the places in question.

TOURIST INFORMATION

⋏	Camp Site		Nature reserve
	Caravan Site	☆	Other tourist feature
ℹ	Information Centre		Preserved railway
P	Parking Facilities		Racecourse
	Viewpoint		Wildlife park
✗	Picnic site		Museum
	Golf course or links		Nature or forest trail
	Castle	m	Ancient monument
	Cave		Telephones : public or motoring organisations
	Country park	PC	Public Convenience
	Garden	▲	Youth Hostel
	Historic house		

◆ ◆ ◆ ◆ Waymarked Path / Long Distance Path / Recreational Path

ORIENTATION

True North
At the centre of the area is 1°16′E of Grid North

Magnetic North
At the centre of the area is about 5°W of Grid North in 1989 decreasing by about ½° in three years

Diagrammatic Only

KEY-MAP 1:625,000 or 10 MILES to 1″

ROAD INFORMATION

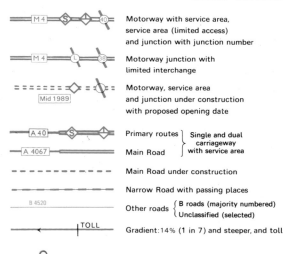

Motorway with service area, service area (limited access) and junction with junction number

Motorway junction with limited interchange

Motorway, service area and junction under construction with proposed opening date

Primary routes } Single and dual carriageway

Main Road } with service area

Main Road under construction

Narrow Road with passing places

Other roads { B roads (majority numbered) / Unclassified (selected)

Gradient:14% (1 in 7) and steeper, and toll

Primary routes and main roads }

Motorways

Primary Routes

These form a national network of recommended through routes which complement the motorway system. Selected places of major traffic importance are known as Primary Route Destinations and are shown on these maps thus BRECON. This relates to the directions on road signs which on Primary Routes have a green background. To travel on a Primary Route, follow the direction to the next Primary Destination shown on the green backed road signs. On these maps Primary Route road numbers and mileages are shown in green.

Motorways

A similar situation occurs with motorway routes where numbers and mileages, shown in blue on these maps correspond to the blue background of motorway road signs.

Mileages are shown on the map between large markers and between small markers in large and small type

1 mile = 1·61 kilometres

GENERAL FEATURES

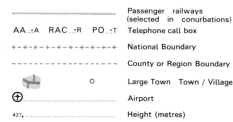

Passenger railways (selected in conurbations)

AA..A RAC..R PO..T Telephone call box

National Boundary

County or Region Boundary

Large Town Town / Village

Airport

427. Height (metres)

WATER FEATURES

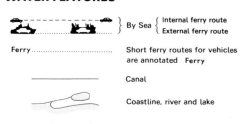

By Sea { Internal ferry route / External ferry route

Ferry Short ferry routes for vehicles are annotated Ferry

Canal

Coastline, river and lake

ATLAS 1:200,000 or 3 MILES to 1"
TOURS 1:250,000 or 4 MILES to 1"

ROADS   Not necessarily rights of way

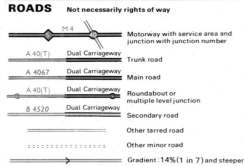

M 4	Motorway with service area and junction with junction number
A 40(T) Dual Carriageway	Trunk road
A 4067 Dual Carriageway	Main road
A 40(T) Dual Carriageway	Roundabout or multiple level junction
B 4520 Dual Carriageway	Secondary road
	Other tarred road
	Other minor road
	Gradient : 14% (1 in 7) and steeper

RAILWAYS

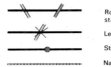

	Road crossing under or over standard gauge track
	Level crossing
	Station
	Narrow gauge track

WATER FEATURES

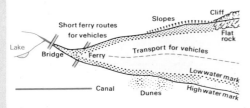

ANTIQUITIES

	Native fortress
	Roman road (course of)
Castle ·	Other antiquities
CANOVIVM ·	Roman antiquity

GENERAL FEATURES

	Buildings	⊕ Civil aerodrome (with custom facilities)
	Wood	Radio or TV mast
		Lighthouse
	Telephones : public or motoring organisations	

RELIEF

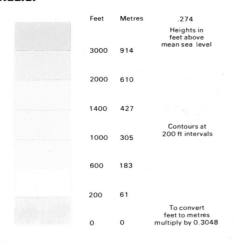

Feet	Metres	.274
		Heights in feet above mean sea level
3000	914	
2000	610	
1400	427	
1000	305	Contours at 200 ft intervals
600	183	
200	61	
0	0	To convert feet to metres multiply by 0.3048

WALKS 1:25,000 or 2½" to 1 MILE
ROADS AND PATHS Not necessarily rights of way

M 4	M 4	Motorway
A 40(T)	A 40(T)	Trunk road
A 4067	A 4067	Main road
B 4520	B 4520	Secondary road
A 40(T)	A 40(T)	Dual carriageway

Narrow roads with passing places are annotated

	Road generally over 4m wide
	Road generally under 4m wide
	Other road, drive or track
....	Path

RAILWAYS

	Multiple track		Level crossing
	Single track		Cutting
	Narrow Gauge		Embankment
	Road over & under		Tunnel
	Siding		

GENERAL FEATURES

Church or Chapel	with tower / with spire / without tower or spire	Electricity transmission line pylon pole
	Gravel pit	NT National Trust always open
	Sand pit	NT National Trust opening restricted
	Chalk pit, clay pit or quarry	FC Forestry Commission pedestrians only (observe local signs)
	Refuse or slag heap	National Park

HEIGHTS AND ROCK FEATURES

Contours are at various metres / feet vertical intervals

50 ·	Determined	ground survey
285 ·	by	air survey

Surface heights are to the nearest metre / foot above mean sea level. Heights shown close to a triangulation pillar refer to the station height at ground level and not necessarily to the summit .

Vertical Face

Loose rock	Boulders	Outcrop	Scree

75
60
50

PUBLIC RIGHTS OF WAY

Public rights of way shown in this guide may not be evident on the ground

----------	Public Paths	Footpath
— — —		Bridleway
+++++		By-way open to all traffic
+-+-+-		Road used as a public path

Public rights of way indicated by these symbols have been derived from Definitive Maps as amended by later enactments or instruments held by Ordnance Survey between 1st Aug 1980 and 1st Oct 1986 and are shown subject to the limitations imposed by the scale of mapping (Note: some walk maps do not show rights of way symbols)
Later information may be obtained from the appropriate County Council.

The representation on these maps of any other road, track or path is no evidence of the existence of a right of way.

WALKS AND TOURS (All Scales)

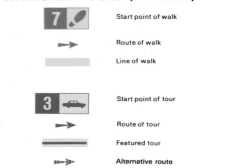

7	Start point of walk
→	Route of walk
	Line of walk
3	Start point of tour
→	Route of tour
	Featured tour
⇢⇢	Alternative route

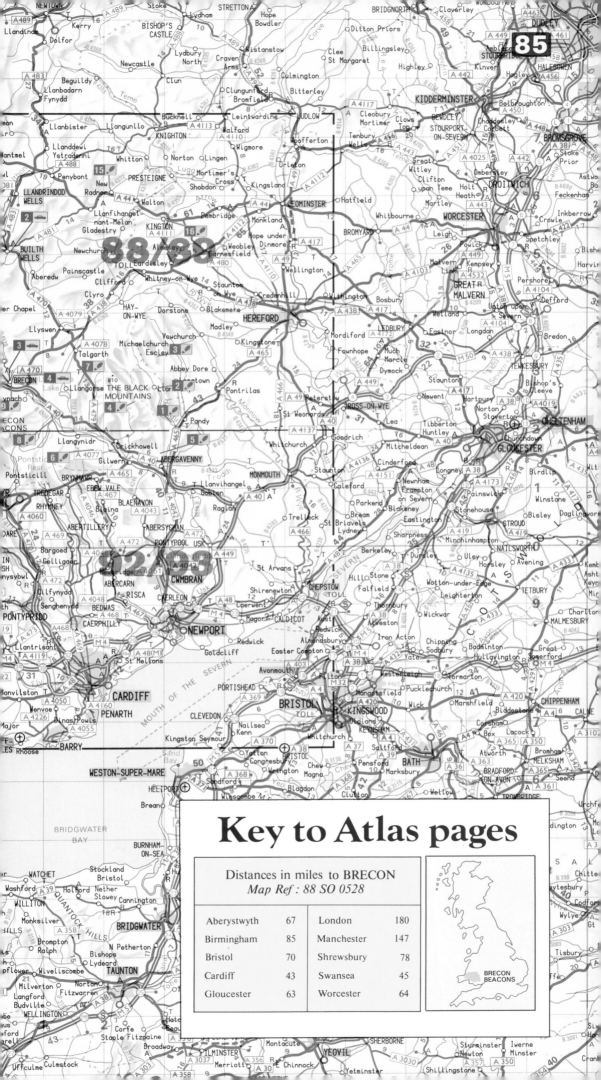

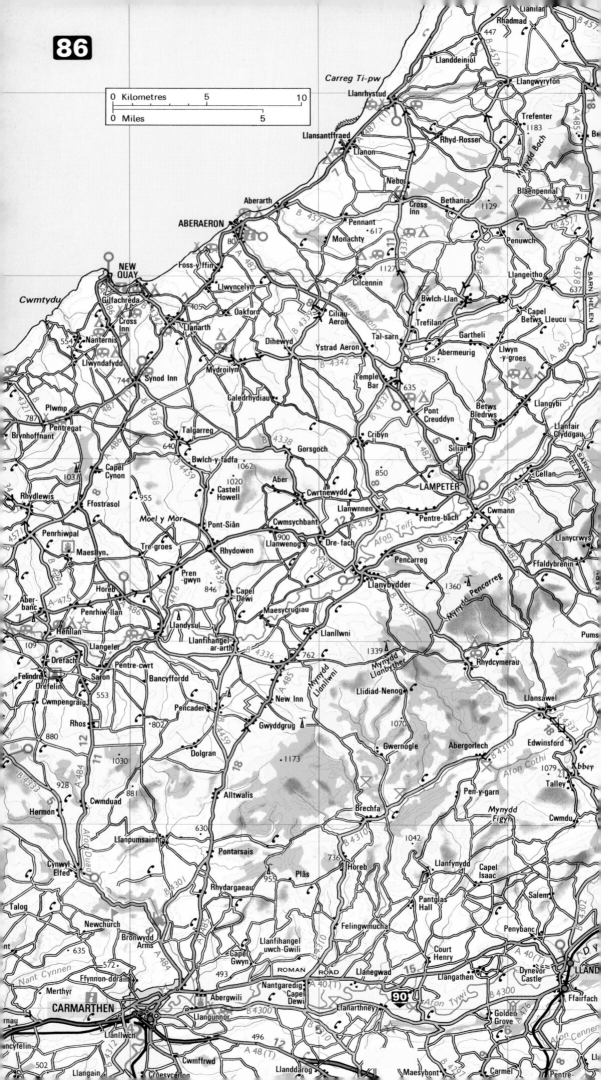

TOUR 1 52 MILES
The New Lakes of Wales

Massive reservoirs, plunging valleys and crashing waterfalls are features of this tour, which also includes visits to a steam railway and a 19th-century mine brought back to life.

The drive commences at Rhayader (see page 67), a small but important market town picturesquely situated in the Upper Wye Valley.

From the Clock Tower leave by the Elan Valley road, B4518. In 3 miles keep forward on an unclassified road and ascend to reach the Caban-coch Reservoir and Dam. This is the first in a chain of reservoirs built between 1892 and 1952 to supply water to Birmingham and the West Midlands. The water was fed out from the reservoir and carried to Birmingham by means of an aqueduct 73½ miles long.

Follow the shoreline for a mile to reach the Garreg-ddu Viaduct. From here a detour can be made by crossing the viaduct to visit the Claerwen Reservoir, the most recently constructed and largest in the Elan Valley system. This diversion involves a five mile drive through attractive woodland before entering a wild and rocky valley towards the end. Near Claerwen is the site of the submerged house of Cwm Elan, where Shelley visited his cousin Thomas Grove after being expelled from Oxford in 1811. The dam wall towers 184ft above the river bed, and is one of the highest gravity dams in Britain.

The main drive continues alongside the Garreg-ddu Reservoir. At the far end bear left across the bridge and climb the winding ascent to the Pen-y-garreg Dam. Follow the Pen-y-garreg Reservoir for almost 2 miles to reach the final reservoir in the system, Craig Goch. There are excellent views of the water here, as the road passes through pleasant moorland scenery.

Three miles beyond the Craig Goch Dam ascend to a T-junction and turn left on to the Aberystwyth road. This former coach road continues along the wide and open moorland valley of the Afon Elan, eventually climbing to a summit of 1,320ft. After crossing the county boundary in to Dyfed the road becomes narrower on the long descent through the deep and wild Ystwyth Valley. The extensive remains of old lead and silver mines are then passed before reaching Cwmystwyth.

After leaving the village ascend and bear right with the Devil's Bridge road, B4574. A climb is then made through well-wooded countryside before passing beneath a stone arch beside a picnic area. The arch was built to commemorate the Jubilee of King George III.

A descent is then made to reach Devil's Bridge. This is the terminus of British Rail's only all-steam-powered operation, the Vale of Rheidol narrow gauge railway, which covers the 12 miles from Aberystwyth in just over an hour. Its name is taken from the three bridges which span the deep Mynach Gorge, with its fine waterfalls dropping 210ft through a rocky chasm. The origin of the lowest bridge, first described by Giraldus Cambrensis in 1188, is unknown; called 'Pont y Gŵr Drwg' (Bridge of the Evil Man) in Welsh, it is traditionally ascribed to the Devil, but could in fact have been constructed by the Knights Hospitallers. Above it are the 1758 bridge and the modern steel road bridge.

Here the drive turns right on to the Ponterwyd road, A4120, and crosses the Devil's Bridge. The road now heads northwards high above the Rheidol Valley, and proceeds to Ponterwyd. On reaching the junction with the A44 a 1½ mile detour to the left along the Aberystwyth road may be taken to visit the Llywernog Silver-Lead Mine. This mid-19th-century mine has been restored to provide interpretive facilities describing the bygone mining industry of the region. There is also a waymarked trail and an audio-visual unit, among other items of interest.

The main tour turns right on to the A44, signed Llangurig. A long, gradual climb is followed up the Castell Valley to Eisteddfa Gurig. This hamlet lies at 1,400ft and is the starting point of the path to Plynlimon (2,470ft), the source of the Rivers Wye and Severn, away to the left.

There now follows a gradual descent, later joining the Upper Wye Valley and passing through Llangurig, 900ft above sea level. This pretty village has a fine restored monastic church which includes the base of a tower built in the 12th century, as well as parts of a 13th-century lancet window, in the south wall of the nave. Its window and details of the rood screen date from the 15th century.

Here follow the road, signed Rhayader, to join the A470. The final nine miles of the drive to Rhayader follow the valley of the River Wye between craggy hills.

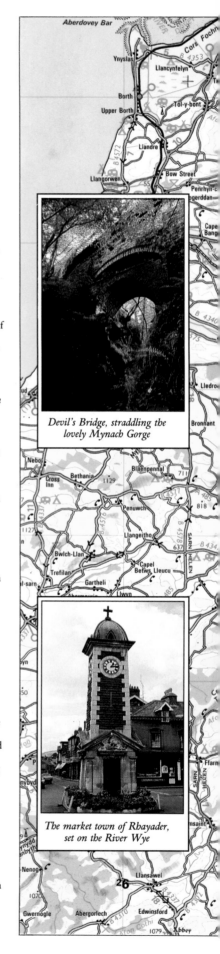

Devil's Bridge, straddling the lovely Mynach Gorge

The market town of Rhayader, set on the River Wye

Caban-coch is the first in a series of reservoirs, built to feed water to Birmingham and the West Midlands in the 19th and 20th centuries

TOUR 2
65 MILES

A Journey to the Marcherlands

This drive takes in the beautiful pastoral scenery of the Welsh borderlands, includes Hay-on-Wye, the ideal town for booklovers, and takes in spectacular mountain views.

The drive starts at Builth Wells (see page 42), a pleasant market town on the River Wye and a former inland resort with saline and sulphur wells. The Royal Welsh Agricultural Show is held here annually.

Follow signs for Brecon to leave by the A470. This road follows the tree-lined River Wye between 1,400ft hills and later passes through Erwood to Llyswen. The name Erwood is a corruption of 'Y Rhyd' – Welsh for 'the ford' which cattle drovers once crossed on their journey over the Wye to England.

At Llyswen keep forward with the A479, signed Abergavenny, and in just over ½ mile bear right and ascend. There are good views ahead towards the Black Mountains before reaching the junction with the A438.

At this junction turn right and enter Bronllys, then turn left following the A479, still signed Abergavenny. Half a mile further, on the left, are the remains of Bronllys Castle which dates from about 1200 and stands, with its single round tower, on a mound surrounded by trees – evidence of the need for strong defence at the northern end of the gap between the Usk and Wye valleys. Other fortified towers in the area are found in Talgarth and Scethrog.

In ¾ mile, at the outskirts of Talgarth, turn left on to the A4078, signed Hereford (A438). Talgarth church contains a 14th-century sepulchral slab, where Hywel Harris, one of the leading figures of Welsh Calvinistic dissent, is buried (see page 70).

After another 2¼ miles turn right at the T-junction to join the A438 and pass through Three Cocks (Aberllyfni). One mile beyond the village go forward with the B4350 along the Wye Valley to visit Hay-on-Wye. This attractive market town, with old buildings and pretty streets, on the English border between the river and the Black Mountains is remarkable for the number and variety of its second-hand book shops. The 12th-century castle of Hay is now mostly in ruins, but during the turbulent days of border disputes the feudal marcher lords would ride out from this spot.

In the town turn left on to the B4351, signed Clyro, and cross the River Wye. In 1¼ miles bear right across the main road on to an unclassified road and enter Clyro. In Clyro the slight remains of a Norman castle built by William de Braöse can be seen.

At the church turn left, signed Painscastle, then in ½ mile turn left again and start a long ascent. Half a mile further bear right and continue the climb across the Clyro Hills before proceeding to Painscastle. Here the remains of a traditional early Norman motte and bailey castle is ascribed to Payn de Quercis (1130); the castle features an extensive keep surrounded by deep double earth banks.

In the village turn right on to the B4594, signed Newchurch. Pass through the secluded communities of Rhos-goch and Newchurch, then continue with the secondary road amid hilly Welsh Marches scenery to Gladestry. *In 2¼ miles bear right and 1 mile further, with views ahead of the Stanner Rocks, turn left on to the A44, signed Rhayader.* Beyond Walton the route by-passes New Radnor and gradually climbs on to the upland area known as Radnor Forest, the highest summits of which – the Black Mixen and Great Rhos – rise to over 2,000ft on the right. This has never been a wood in the modern sense; in medieval times 'forest' meant unenclosed land used for hunting. The north side is now heavily planted with conifers almost to the skyline and the valley contains the alarmingly named Water-Break-Its-Neck waterfall with a 90ft plunge.

Continue to Penybont and on to Crossgates. Here, turn left at the roundabout with the A483, signed Llandrindod. The valley of the River Ithon is then followed for the short distance to Llandrindod Wells. This pleasant Victorian and Edwardian spa town is the county town of Powys (an amalgamation of the old counties of Montgomeryshire, Breconshire and Radnorshire). Its springs were found to have 'healing powers' in the 18th century, but the town really came into its own with the advent of the railway. A local museum and a Welsh Crafts Centre are among its modern features.

Remain on the A483, signed Builth Wells. After 7 miles, at the roundabout, take the first exit and shortly cross the River Wye for the return journey to Builth Wells.

A Norman stronghold captured by the Welsh: Bronllys Castle

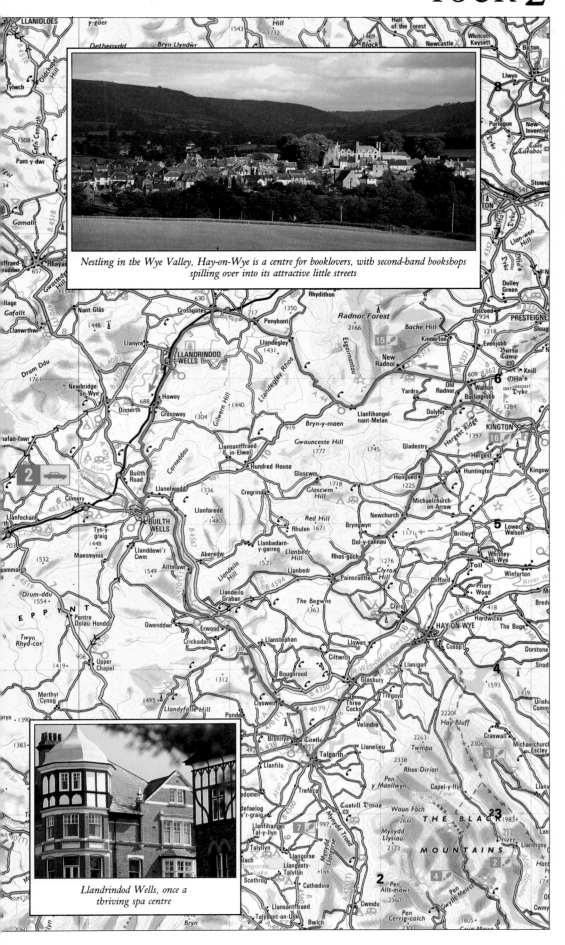

Nestling in the Wye Valley, Hay-on-Wye is a centre for booklovers, with second-hand bookshops spilling over into its attractive little streets

Llandrindod Wells, once a thriving spa centre

TOUR 3

Mynydd Eppynt & Llyn Brianne

This drive uses narrow and winding roads in places – with unprotected drops. Although these provide spectacular views they may be unsuitable for nervous drivers or passengers.

The drive starts in Brecon, a town full of interesting reminders of its 700-year history.

Follow High Street Superior B4520 (not shown), signed Brecon Cathedral. In ¼ mile turn left, signed Upper Chapel, and shortly pass Brecon Cathedral on the right. This 13th-century building was designated a cathedral in 1923, and overlooks the River Honddu.

Continue through pleasant hill scenery following the Honddu Valley, later passing through Pwllgloyw and Lower Chapel to reach Upper Chapel. In ½ mile turn left on to the B4519, signed Llangammarch Wells. This road may be closed occasionally, as it passes through an army firing range. An alternative route is to remain on the B4520 to Builth Wells and then to follow signs to Llandovery (A483) to Llanwrtyd Wells. The main drive crosses the upland moorland area of Mynydd Eppynt, and from the 1,500ft summit there are fine views to the north across the Irfon Valley.

At the foot of the descent turn left at the crossroads on to an unclassified road to reach Llangammarch Wells. Placed at the confluence of the Rivers Irfon and Cammarch, this village has springs containing barium chloride, said to be especially effective in heart diseases.

Bear right to cross the River Irfon, then pass beneath the railway and turn left, signed Llanwrtyd Wells. In ¾ mile turn left and continue along this by-road for a further 3½ miles before turning left again, on to the A483, to enter Llanwrtyd Wells (see page 59). Here there are iron and sulphur springs; the old village, with its parish church, is further up the valley from the modern settlement.

Here turn right, unclassified, signed Abergwesyn and follow the wooded Irfon Valley (narrow road in places). In 1¼ miles cross the river, then turn right. A number of picnic sites are passed before reaching the hamlet of Abergwesyn.

The drive turns left here, signed Tregaron, and continues up the valley along a narrow road, passing through open and dramatic scenery. The Irfon is crossed three more times before the ascent of the Devil's Staircase (1 in 4, with hairpin bends). After the 1,550ft summit there is a 1 in 4 descent before turning left, signed Llandovery. The drive now continues through the extensive Tywi (or Towy) Forest and in 2 miles it starts to run high above the Llyn Brianne Reservoir. This well engineered road follows a winding forest route for some 4 miles, with occasional glimpses of Llyn Brianne. The spectacular reservoir, dammed by a 300ft-high wall of rocks, occupies a once-remote part of the country rich in wildlife. Before the existence of the reservoir local inhabitants would travel on horseback to the adjacent Camddwr Valley, where the chapel of Soar-y-Mynydd was situated halfway between Rhandirmwyn and Tregaron. It was so difficult to reach that visiting preachers had to stay in a small house built alongside the chapel, with a stable attached.

Later, open moorland is crossed before making a long descent in order to pass a turning (on the right) to the 300ft-high Llyn Brianne Dam and viewing point. The main drive continues descending into the attractive Tywi Valley. A mile beyond Llyn Brianne is Ystradffin, a place associated with the Welsh Robin Hood, Twm Siôn Catti, whose hide-out can be seen by following a nature trail alongside the Tywi (see page 67). Rhandirmwyn, a village set around the bend of the river and once an important lead-mining centre, is a good starting point for exploring the valley. There are still surface workings and ruins to be seen nearby.

Later, approaching Llandovery, turn right and immediately left across the main road (signed Brecon) to enter the town centre, then turn left on to the A40 (not shown). Shortly join the deep, wooded valley of the Afon Gwydderig for a long, gradual ascent. After 2½ miles pass the 'Coachman's Cautionary' – a monument set in a lay-by on the right (see page 56).

Beyond Trecastle the Upper Usk Valley is joined for Sennybridge. Sennybridge was mainly developed in the 19th century, when it took hold of the sheep and cattle market once held in Defynnog, before the turnpike road was opened.

Remain on the Brecon road (A40), and in six miles pass a picnic site beside the Usk (on the left). Shortly, skirt Llanspyddid and in 1¼ miles at the roundabout take the first exit, B4601, for the return to Brecon.

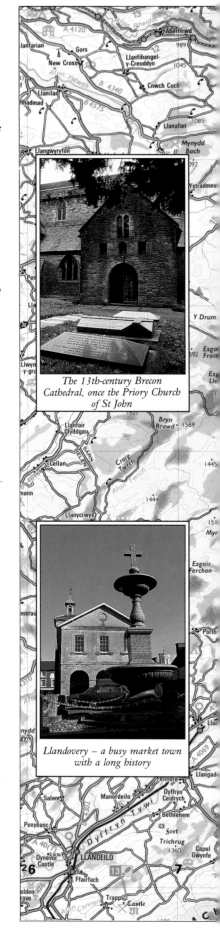

The 13th-century Brecon Cathedral, once the Priory Church of St John

Llandovery – a busy market town with a long history

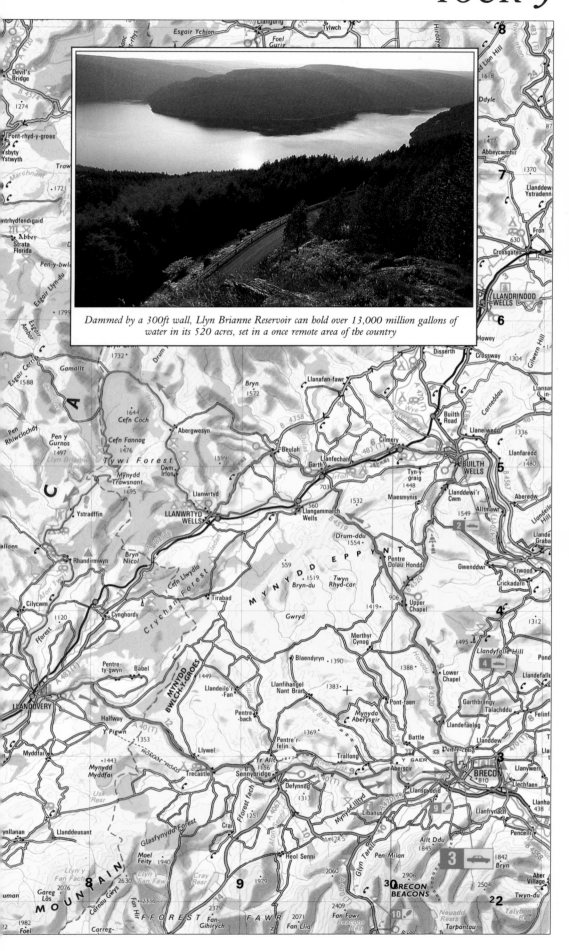

Dammed by a 300ft wall, Llyn Brianne Reservoir can hold over 13,000 million gallons of water in its 520 acres, set in a once remote area of the country

TOUR 4 65 MILES

The Brecon Beacons & the Usk Valley

Several different features of the Welsh landscape are taken in during this drive – including sweeping mountain roads, the head of the South Wales Valleys, and natural and man-made lakes.

The drive starts at Brecon (see page 40), the main centre for touring the Brecon Beacons National Park.

Leave by the B4601, signed Cardiff (A470), and in 1 mile at the roundabout take the second exit on to the A470. Proceed to Libanus and ¼ mile beyond the church turn right, unclassified, signed Mountain Centre. After 1½ miles turn right to visit the Brecon Beacons Mountain Centre. The Centre provides an introduction to the geology and natural history of the Beacons and nearby Black Mountains.

From the entrance return to the road junction and turn right (no sign), then follow a narrow by-road for ½ mile to a T-junction. Here turn left and continue along another narrow road, with views of the Brecon Beacons to the left. After 1¾ miles turn left on to the A4215 (still no sign). In just over ½ mile turn left again. The drive then gradually descends into the Tarell Valley, with more views ahead of the Beacons.

On reaching the A470 turn right, signed Merthyr Tydfil, and follow the long ascent (with Fan Fawr, 2,409ft high, ahead) to the summit at 1,440ft. There follows a descent along the Taf Valley, passing three reservoirs.

A turning on the right before the last reservoir leads to the Garwnant Forest Centre beside Llwyn-on Reservoir. Continue to Cefn-coed-y-cymmer, on the outskirts of Merthyr Tydfil. Here turn left on to an unclassified road, signed Talybont. Alternatively, keep forward with the A470 for a short diversion to visit the 19th-century Cyfarthfa Castle and Museum at Merthyr Tydfil. This was the home of the Crawshays, who took over the Cyfarthfa Ironworks. It was started in 1766 and employed 1,500 men by the turn of the century.

The main tour continues through a quarrying area, later keeping left before proceeding to Pontsticill. Remain on the Talybont road and beyond the village bear left. The turning on the right leads across the Pontsticill Reservoir down to the Brecon Mountain Railway Centre. The drive now heads northwards through the wooded Taf Fechan Valley to follow a narrower road alongside the shore of Pontsticill Reservoir.

After 1¾ miles turn left, then in another mile turn right and descend. Pass the Taf Fechan Picnic Site and ascend on to higher ground, then descend through attractive woodland to follow the valley of the Caerfanell River. Continue alongside the Talybont Reservoir and at the far end pass the dam. In 1¼ miles bear right and almost ½ mile further cross the Monmouthshire and Brecon Canal by a lift-bridge, then turn right on to the B4558 (not shown) to enter Talybont-on-Usk. At the far end keep forward with the Crickhowell road along the Usk Valley. At Llangynidr turn right on to the B4560, signed Beaufort. The drive now ascends, with hairpin bends, to a summit at 1,460ft. From here there are magnificent views across the Usk Valley to the Black Mountains.

Beyond the quarry turn left on to an unclassified road, signed Llangattock. A gradual descent is then made to re-enter the Usk Valley at Llangattock. Cross the hump-back bridge and turn left in to the village. Later turn left again on to the A4077 (not shown) then at the the traffic signals turn right and cross the River Usk. On the far side bear left (signed Brecon A40) for the edge of Crickhowell. This small country town contains some Georgian houses, a restored 14th-century church and some remains of a ruined 13th-century castle.

Leave by the Brecon road, A40, to follow the north side of the Usk Valley. After 1½ miles the A479 (to the right) may be taken to visit Tretower where there are the ruins of a 13th-century castle as well as Tretower Court. The castle's huge, single round tower can still be seen looming over the fields.

The main tour continues with the A40 and eventually ascends to Bwlch, a good Usk Valley viewpoint. Beyond the village turn right on to the B4560, signed Llangorse. Later, to the left of this road, is Llangorse Lake – the second largest natural lake in Wales.

Pass through Llangorse village and near the end turn left, unclassified, signed Brecon. Shortly, to the left, is the turning which leads to the lakeside.

In ¾ mile keep left and continue to Llanfihangel Tal-y-llyn. Keep left in to the village and at the end bear right. In 2¼ miles, at the T-junction, turn left, pass under the bridge and turn right to join the A40. After another ¾ mile, at the roundabout, take the second exit on to the B4601 for the return to Brecon.

Llangorse Lake offers boating, fishing and wonderful scenery

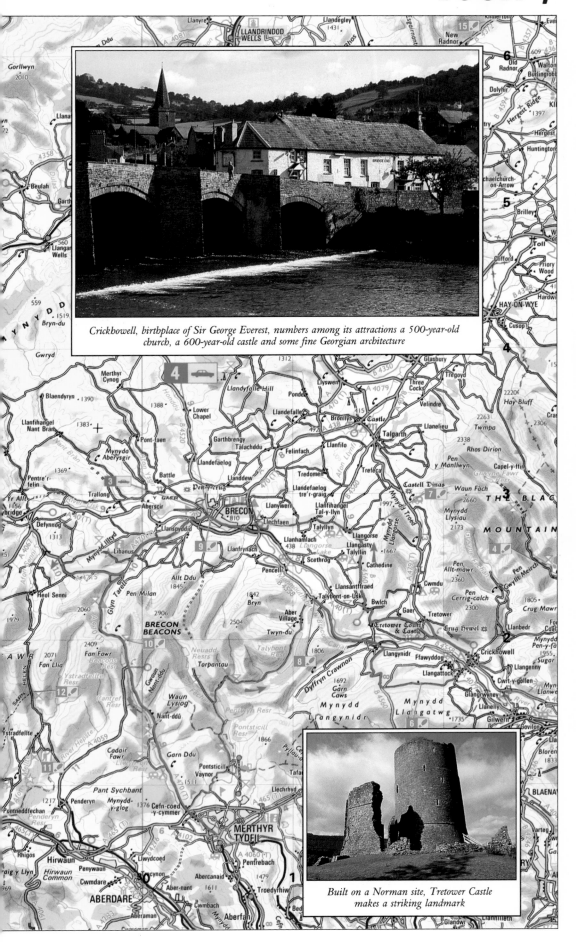

Crickhowell, birthplace of Sir George Everest, numbers among its attractions a 500-year-old church, a 600-year-old castle and some fine Georgian architecture

Built on a Norman site, Tretower Castle makes a striking landmark

WALK 1

Cwmyoy Church in the Vale of Ewyas

Allow 2½ hours

The U-shaped Vale of Ewyas, more familiarly known as the Llanthony Valley, was shaped by a glacier. This walk provides views into the valley from its western ridge and visits the leaning church of Cwmyoy – a memorable experience in itself. It can be very wet in places and boots are advisable.

Park at the car park, just above the Queen's Head Inn (SO312222), where a small charge may be requested if you are not purchasing refreshments. Follow the lane uphill above the inn to enjoy views to the left of Skirrid Fawr and Bryn Arw. On passing Pen-rhiw cottage the gradient decreases and later the road becomes a cart track. Go through a gate to gain the open hillside. At this point a detour may be made to the left to inspect the ditches and ramparts of Gaer Hill fort. This fine example of a fortified Iron Age British camp is oval and encloses about 4½ acres.

Carry on along the track which now crosses a bracken covered hillside. After passing a Forestry plantation on the right the views start to open out. Across the valley can be seen the sandstone cliffs above Cwmyoy. In the distance is Bâl Mawr, and to the left can be seen the Grwyne Fawr Valley. Above it, far ahead, is the table-top summit of Pen y Gader Fawr.

On the right pass a massive stone slab stile, a feature frequently seen in this area. Go through the gate set in

a wall on the right (about 200yds before an isolated cottage) and follow a bridlepath across a field to enter a Forestry plantation through a hunting gate. Now follow a stony track through the trees, descending into the Vale of Ewyas. This track may be muddy in places, for it is often used by pony trekkers.

On reaching a forest road turn left and go almost immediately right to continue down the bridlepath, which twists and turns down the hillside to reach a hunting gate. At the point where the path emerges from the trees there is a good view across the valley to the church of Cwmyoy.

Go through a gate and follow the track, which curves around to the right to reach another gate and then continues as a holly-lined tunnel. Where it meets a road, go straight across, over a stile and diagonally across a field to reach another stile beside a bridge. Turn right and follow a road for about ¼ mile. Shortly after passing another stone slab stile, turn left up a track leading directly to Cwmyoy church. St Martin's is about 700 years old and appears to be toppling over; the tower leans towards the hillside and the chancel tilts towards the valley. At some time in its history subsidence disturbed the foundations.

Leave the churchyard, go through a gate and turn right, then right again down a road, passing on the right an old stone cider press. At a T-junction turn left and follow the lane through the green valley of Ewyas for about ¾ mile. Ahead can be seen Skirrid Fawr, otherwise known as the Holy Mountain, the setting for several legends. The notch at its northern end is said to have been caused by the earthquake at the Crucifixion. Its English name could derive from this legend – or from St Michael's Chapel, a place of pilgrimage which once stood on the summit.

At a corner of a field on the right cross a stile and go diagonally across a field, over a stream (no footbridge) and then across the next field to walk beside the Afon Honddu. Pass over a small footbridge and then carry on to reach a gate. Turn right, following the road over a two-arched stone bridge, and return to your starting point.

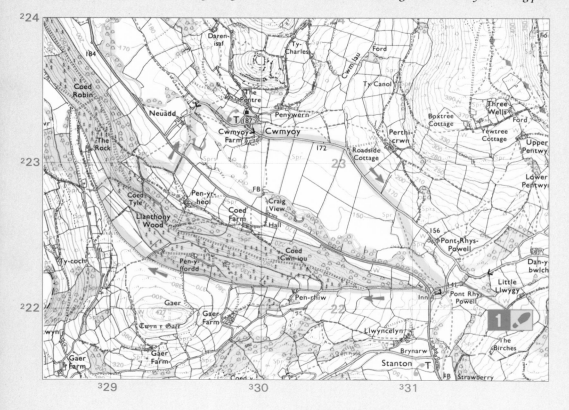

A Bird's Eye View of Llanthony Priory

Allow 3 hours

Llanthony Priory, in the beautiful Vale of Ewyas, is an historic and noble ruin, and its situation is best appreciated from the hills above. The summit of Bâl Mawr provides extensive views of the heather-covered ridges of the Black Mountains.

From Llanthony Priory car park (SO289278) walk down the drive, passing St David's Church, and go over a stile. Cross a field and keep left of an old stone barn, which was originally the priory gatehouse. Turn right along the road to pass the Half Moon Inn and go left at the next junction, crossing two bridges in rapid succession. At the top of a short rise, turn left up a track, following a stony path between steep banks (often wet underfoot). Go through a gate and then on between two stone walls. Pass through a hunting gate and turn right to follow the fence. From here there are good views up the valley towards Capel-y-ffin and Darren Llwyd, rising above the hamlet.

Go through another gate where there are views down into the beautiful valley. The 12th-century chronicler, Giraldus Cambrensis, who recorded his journeys through Wales, once described this valley as 'an arrow shot broad'.

On reaching a fork in the track go left and follow a diagonal path which makes an elbow bend and then heads up the bracken covered slope in a southerly direction. Across the valley notice the old quarry directly above the priory. Stone was obtained here for building purposes and the quarry probably supplied stone for the priory itself. At a corner pause for a bird's eye view of the priory and Llanthony hamlet. This name is a corruption of Llan Ddewi Nant Hodni (Honddu) – meaning The Church of St David on the River Honddu. According to tradition, the first church was erected here in the 6th century by St David, who was declared the patron saint of Wales 600 years later. The priory was founded in 1102 by the Augustine Order but the monks did not stay very long; they considered the valley inhospitable and left to found a new priory at Gloucester, which they also called Llanthony (see page 58).

The track flattens out for a while and passes above Cwm Bwchel. Ahead, and slightly to the right, can be seen the summit of Bâl Mawr. Where the track divides, keep to the right in order to avoid a boggy area and then head up towards a prominent cairn on the skyline. On reaching the cairn turn right and follow a track up to the summit of Bâl Mawr, marked by a trig' point, to enjoy an extensive view. *Return to the cairn on the col below and follow the track down to the head of Cwm Bwchel. When the track divides follow the path leading down the left side of the cwm. It soon descends into the narrow valley and becomes a stony track.* This must have been a medieval approach route to the priory from the Grwyne Fawr Valley on the west side of the ridge. Once more, delightful views of the beautifully situated priory may be appreciated.

Head down to a stile and shortly cross another one into a field. Continue through a farmyard, passing through two gates, and descend between two streams to reach a hunting gate. Cross a footbridge and follow the stream down to a stile. Shortly, cross another stile into a field and then go on beside the stream to reach a stile and a footbridge. Llanthony hamlet is just around the corner.

WALK 3
Along the Cat's Back and Down the Olchon Valley

Allow 2 hours

The narrow and most easterly ridge of the Black Mountains is called Crib y Garth, but is more popularly known by its English name – 'the Cat's Back'.

Just to the north of Little Black Hill and at the foot of the Cat's Back is a small car park and picnic site which is the starting point for this walk (SO288328). Go over a stile and head up the hillside following a well defined path, which is quite steep at first. When the ridge is gained, the walking becomes easier. On the left can be seen the Hatterrall Ridge, which is the route of the Offa's Dyke Long Distance Path.

The ridge becomes stepped and rocky. It then narrows for a short distance before broadening into Black Hill

where the summit is marked by a trig' point at 640 metres. Birds likely to be seen on this hill are the buzzard, distinguished by its broad, rounded wings, short tail and soaring flight; the little brown meadow pipit; or the skylark, uttering its warbling song. The ring ouzel may be spotted in spring and summer and very often large flocks of lapwings, or peewits, can be seen during late summer and autumn. In the distance is Hay Bluff, otherwise known as Pen-y-Beacon, and to its left is Y Twmpa, often referred to as Lord Hereford's Knob. Below, to the right, is the Monnow Valley and the tiny hamlet of Craswall which has a quaint old pub called the Bull's Head and a simple church; and in a secluded valley known as Fox Dingle can be found the scanty remains of a priory founded in the reign of King John.

Follow a well-trodden path in a north westerly direction towards Hay Bluff, until the head of the Olchon Valley is reached. Turn left here and follow a track descending into the valley. On reaching a road, turn left and follow it back to a junction where a turning leads up to Black Hill car park.

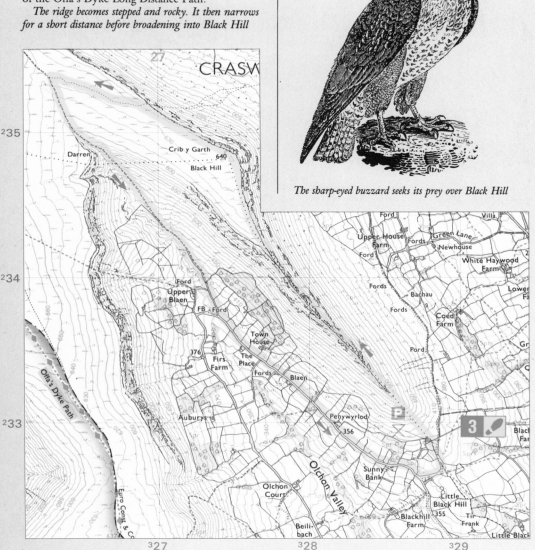

The sharp-eyed buzzard seeks its prey over Black Hill

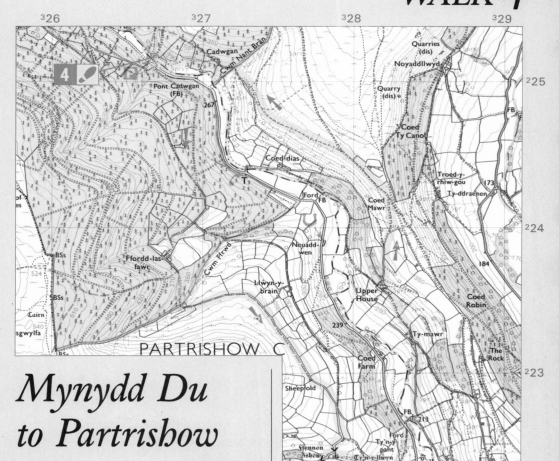

Mynydd Du to Partrishow

Allow 3½ hours

The Grwyne Fawr Valley passes through the heart of the Black Mountains and contains the forest of Mynydd Du. This walk takes in both sides of the valley and includes a visit to the secluded little church of Partrishow, well known for its beautiful carved rood screen.

Start at the Mynydd Du Forestry Commission car park at Pont Cadwgan in the Grwyne Fawr Valley (SO267252). From the car park go straight across the road and follow a forest drive to ascend gently through the woods. On reaching a cleared area, and the junction of tracks, bear left. The views open up now to encompass the Grwyne Fawr Valley below and Gaer Hill Iron Age fort ahead.

Continue past plantations of fir trees, through a gate and on past Ffordd-las-fawr farmhouse. The track leads on to the edge of the forest at Cwm Ffrwd. Go through a hunting gate, ford the stream and continue beside a stone wall. Views can be enjoyed now across the valley with the prominent cairn of Garn Wen and the sharp ridge of Chwarel-y-Fan being noticeable features.

At a gate the track descends to join a road. Turn right here, descend into the Nant Mair Valley, and go over a stile on the left. Below is the little church of St Partricio (Partrishow). Situated at about 1,000ft above sea level, this neat little church, dedicated to St Issui, contains a beautiful 15th-century carved oak screen. On the wall is a skeleton with scythe and hour glass, which is reputed to have been painted in human blood.

Leave the church through a gate at the eastern end of the churchyard and cross a field to join a track leading down past Ty'n-y-llwyn farmhouse. This farm, whose
name means 'the house in the grove', is an attractive 15th-century building.

Immediately after the farmhouse turn left through a gate and cross a field. Then go over a stile and bear right down to another gate in the corner of a field. From there, go diagonally left to pass between two ruined buildings and down to a stile. Cross a road and, shortly, go over a bridge to pass the Tabernacle Baptist Chapel (1837). Follow the lane past Tŷ Mawr to Upper House and continue between the house and a barn to follow the track up to another gate. Look back towards the old farmhouse to see the semi-circular bread oven protruding from the end wall.

The track ascends beside a fence and passes through two gates. Follow a rutted path up to the crest of the ridge. Look down the ridge to observe a small stone pillar about 3ft high which is known as Dial Garreg (the stone of revenge). It is said to mark the scene of an ambush in 1135 when the Norman Marcher Lord, Richard de Clare, and his party were massacred by a band of Welshmen.

Now bear left and follow a track heading towards a stone wall (on the right). Follow a path along the western slopes of the ridge, enjoying views into the valley. It is hard to believe that this valley once echoed with the sound of steam locomotives on a railway leading to the construction site of the Grwyne Fawr Reservoir, which was once the highest reservoir in Britain.

After reaching a track junction go left to traverse the hillside and descend into Cwm Nant Brân. Cross a stream and go through a hunting gate, then go on past Cadwgan farm. Keep left at the next junction and descend through the wood to reach the car park.

Ascent of the Sugar Loaf

Allow 2¾ hours

Separated from the main mass of the Black Mountains by the Grwyne Valley, the Sugar Loaf (or Mynydd Pen-y-Fâl) is one of three peaks dominating Abergavenny. Its shape is eye-catching from every angle.

Start from Llwyn Du car park (SO288166). Go up the farm lane on the left leading to Porth-y-parc farm and continue through the farmyard. Soon the conical summit of the Sugar Loaf, owned by the National Trust, will be seen ahead.

Follow a broad lane between hedges to cross a stile, then go on beside a fence and over another stile. The sunken track provides pleasant views across the Afon Cibi Valley.

Soon the track crosses an open area and another stile is reached. Just beyond this, keep left, passing remnants of a stone wall. Cross two stiles in rapid succession and then go through a gate. At the next junction of tracks keep left. Shortly afterwards, look out for a rock on the left with an Ordnance Survey bench-mark (a wedge-like horizontal notch surmounting a broad arrow) cut into it. Bench-marks indicate an ascertained height or level, and are used as points of reference by surveyors and cartographers.

On reaching another stile, join the Rholben ridge-track at Twyn Gwyn. Keep straight on for a while and then turn right to follow a path to the Sugar Loaf summit, which is about 300yds long. An extensive view ranges from the mass of the Black Mountains to the north and the Usk Valley beyond Crickhowell with the Brecon Beacons in the distance, to Ysgyryd (Skirrid) Fawr and the Malverns and Cotswold Hills in the east.

From the summit, descend with care on the east side and follow a path down to the fence line above the Cibi Valley. Turn left and walk beside the fence, heading for

A pleasant walk leads on to the Sugar Loaf, presented to the National Trust in 1936 by Viscountess Rhondda

the Deri ridge. At a division of tracks keep right, eventually to join the ridge. Now turn right and follow a broad path along the crest of the ridge, keeping right at the next junction. From here there are views of the three peaks: the bulky Blorenge to the south, the jagged ridge of Skirrid Fawr to the east and the conical summit of the Sugar Loaf now behind you.

On reaching Allt (spot height 376) at the end of the highest point of Deri ridge, descend a short slope and at a track junction make a 90° turn to the right. At the next junction take the second track on the left into the woods. 'Deri' is Welsh for oak, which was once used to provide charcoal for the furnaces of the iron works in the Clydach Gorge. The bark also provided tannin for the leather tanning industry.

The track descends with the Blorenge looming in the distance. Go through a gate and, opposite a bungalow, turn sharp right to pass through another gate, then follow a broad track doubling back through the trees. This route provides pleasant views of the Cibi tumbling through the valley.

Continue through another gate. The path narrows, rises slightly, then drops down to join a farm lane. Turn left here and head back to the car park.

WALK 6
A Limestone Escarpment

Allow 2¼ hours

Craig y Cilau, with its amphitheatre of limestone cliffs, screes and trees, is an impressive sight, and Cwm Onneu below often echoes with the sound of the rushing waters of the Onnau Fach.

Park just above a cattle grid on the side of the road which connects Llangattock village with the B4560 (SO183168). Walk up the road a few yards and turn left along a cart track. Go through two gates, then turn right through a gateway and follow a stone wall downhill. Turn left through yet another gateway and pass a ruined barn. Head across a field to a stile, then go across the next field to a gate. From here, cross two more fields and make for the floor of the valley where a track follows the stream. Pass through a gate and follow the track through the valley. This valley provides a peaceful walk, with the dramatic limestone escarpment looming above.

Cross a stile in a wall on the right, then cross a stream on stepping stones. Follow an ascending track to the left, ignoring the lower track by the stream. This track goes around the slope of the hillside, providing impressive views across Cwm Onneu and the Usk Valley to the Black Mountains.

In due course, a 'platform' between two industrial inclines is reached. Here, there was once a brake wheel which controlled the descent of the trams loaded with limestone down the incline into the valley below. The tramroad leads on to meet the canal at Llangattock wharf.

Turn right and ascend the upper incline. Notice the stonework at the top, where the winch house was.

Now follow the tramroad to the right. At this point an extensive view takes in, from right to left: Skirrid Fawr, Sugar Loaf, Gaer Hill, Hatterall

Over 250 botanical species can be found at Craig y Cilau Nature Reserve, and 49 kinds of bird breed there

Ridge, Table Mountain, Pen Cerrig Calch, Castell Dinas, Mynydd Troed, Mynydd Llangorse and Allt-yr-Esgair. Further on, there is a spectacular view across the amphitheatre formed by the escarpment of Craig y Cilau. In 1959 this escarpment and part of the valley below was declared a National Nature Reserve. It contains several caves, rich flora and a number of uncommon trees, including several species of whitebeam. The finest limestone vegetation – the richest type in the Park – is preserved on the Craig y Cilau precipices. It makes a marked contrast with the duller shades of peat vegetation such as matgrass and heather. Just beyond a bay in the cliff is the entrance to Eglwys Faen (stone church) cave, which has several entrances. Mynydd Llangattock is a cavers' paradise, with several large systems still being developed and explored. These include Ogof Agen Allwedd and Ogof Darren Cilau in addition to Eglwys Faen. The total length of passages has been estimated at over 60 miles.

Look out for a narrow path on the right which leaves the quarry track and diagonally descends the hillside below. It keeps parallel with the escarpment, passes through a wooded area and crosses a boulder-strewn slope, to lead across to the left hand side of the mire called Waun Ddu (Black Bog). By the remains of a stone building, follow the track up to a fence. Continue beside the fence and bear left to return to the start.

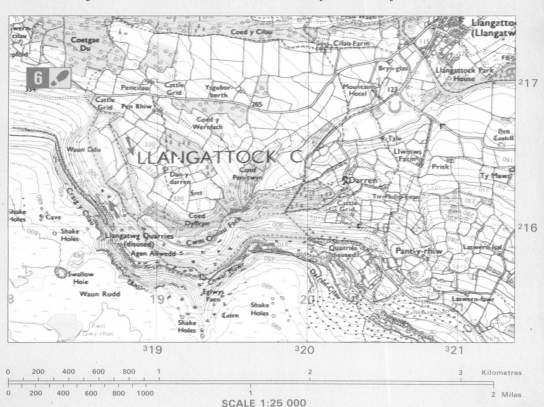

WALK 7

Views of Llangorse Lake, the Beacons and the Black Mountains

Allow 3 hours

A circuit of Mynydd Llangorse provides panoramic views to the largest natural lake and the loftiest mountains in South Wales. At the highest point of the walk, the view takes in the Rhiangoll Valley and the westerly ridges of the Black Mountains.

This walk starts from the summit of the pass in Cwm Sorgwm, where a small parking area is available (SO161283). Follow the path in a southerly direction and head for the fence on the right to pick up a path which leads round the western slopes of Mynydd Llangorse, providing level walking and good views. The hills of Mynydd Llangorse and Allt-yr-Esgair guard Llangorse Lake on the east and south; the other sides are open. Llangorse Lake is the second largest natural lake in Wales and its waters are dammed behind a barrier of glacial gravel. Many legends are associated with it, including the ancient belief that a town is buried beneath its waters. When there is a heavy swell on the lake, some say that the sound of church bells can be heard! Great-crested grebe and other fish-eating birds breed on the lake, white and yellow water lilies can be seen on the water and pikes and eels of remarkable size have been caught there. An old Welsh saying used to be 'cyhyd â llysywen Syfaddan' – 'as long as a Syfaddan eel'. A

feature of special interest is an artificial island in the lake, constructed of stones and held in place by piles. This is marked on the map as Bwlch. Such islands, known as crannogs, are believed to have been used as ancient Celtic dwellings. In 1925 a dug-out canoe, hewn from a single oak log, was found in the lake. Now in the Brecon Museum, it may have provided transport for the island-dwellers.

After two miles or so of steady walking at an altitude of about 350 metres, reach a hunting gate, where the path enters the edge of a wood. It then ascends and crosses a diagonal track. Soon another hunting gate is reached, and from there the path follows a stone wall for a short way. On emerging from the wood, cross a field and go past an isolated cottage named Cwm-Shenkin. Then cross another field to pass through a gate and from there follow a diagonal path leading up the hillside. Curving around to meet a fence, the track then joins the crest of the ridge and a cairn. Turn left here and follow the ridge track for a short distance then fork right along a narrower path. The path skirts around the head of two side valleys and reaches another cairn. From here descend on a zigzag path into Cwm Sorgwm to join a track heading in a northerly direction back up the valley. It joins the road just below the summit of the pass, which completes the circuit. The three stones set in the ground here have names and dates inscribed on them. However, they are not grave stones, as many people who come across them imagine, but boundary stones, marking the junction of three landowners' estates.

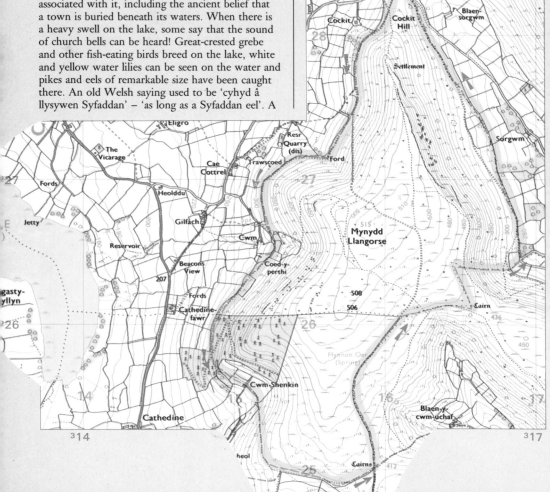

Along the Bryn Oer Tramroad

Allow 3 hours

This route provides an opportunity to walk a short section of the Bryn Oer Tramroad, once an important industrial link between Tredegar and Talybont-on-Usk. There are views of the eastern end of the Brecon Beacons as the walk crosses the ridge above Talybont Reservoir and then returns along the towpath of the Monmouthsire and Brecon Canal.

Park in Talybont-on-Usk village (SO115226) and walk past the side of the White Hart Inn to cross a stone bridge over the canal. From here a lane leads on to join the Bryn Oer Tramroad, passing above the Afon Caerfanell. On crossing another bridge look down to see the track of the old Merthyr to Brecon Railway passing below. This railway opened in 1865 and closed in 1963. From Talybont it climbed steeply for seven miles up to Torpantau, and passed through the highest railway tunnel in Britain.

Continue to the right along the tramroad. Stones set in the ground once held the saddles, or supports, which kept the rails in place. A natural tunnel is formed along here by the trees arching overhead. The Bryn Oer Tramroad was opened in 1815 to carry coal and lime from Brynoer, near

Tafarnaubach, to the canal at Talybont.

The tramroad gently ascends the side of the valley and provides views into the eastern cwms of the Brecon Beacons. Below can be seen the little hamlet of Aberclydach and above looms the summit of Craig Pwllfa. The dam of Talybont Reservoir can also be seen below. Fed by the Afon Caerfanell, this reservoir was constructed in the 1930s to supply water to Newport. Its 318 acres provide excellent fishing; brown and rainbow trout swim here. The reservoir is also a major haunt of winter wildfowl, with a small passage of waders.

Almost level with the dam, a track leads up on the left to a stile. Go over the stile and follow the path up through the trees to reach a field. Continue across the field to a gate, then turn right onto a road by a cattle grid. Cross the road to follow a track to a gate. Cross a sloping field towards a wood. Go through a gate and walk through the next field to join a rutted track. Pass through a gate and then carry on past a gate marked 'Private'. Keep beside the hedge to reach another gate. Cross a stream and go on to a gate at the corner of a wood directly ahead. Shortly afterwards, cross another stream and bear right to go over a stile. Then turn left to join a track leading down to the canal. Cross a girder bridge (which obscures an older stone construction) and a stile on the right, giving access to the canal towpath, which is then followed back to Talybont. A special feature passed on this section of the canal is the Ashford Tunnel. It is about 375yds long and, as there was no towpath in the tunnel, the horses pulling the narrowboats had to be led over the top. The boats were then either 'legged' through by men lying on their backs and 'walking' along the top of the tunnel, or 'shafted' with poles pushed against the walls.

Follow the towpath, to return to the starting point at Talybont-on-Usk.

Waterways between Brecon and Brynich

Allow 3 hours

Views across the Usk Valley and of the old borough town of Brecon – set in the middle of the Brecon Beacons National Park at the confluence of the rivers Usk and Honddu – can be enjoyed on this walk. Brecon is the terminus of the Monmouthshire and Brecon Canal system.

The walk starts in Brecon from a car park on the west side of the river (SO043285). Follow the lane to reach a metal kissing gate, just to the left of a lodge house. Continue beside the river to reach a stile, then go over a small footbridge spanning a tributary stream. Follow a path up to a lane and turn left. The route now passes below the beautiful wooded slopes of Coed Nant-y-ceiliog, providing pleasant views across the valley floor to Brecon and its two Iron Age hill forts of Pen-y-crug and Slwch Tump. The former is a splendid fortress, defended by five ramparts and ditches. Constructed by the Celts in about 100BC it is oval in shape and about ⅓ acre in circumference.

Soon the lane rises beside the A40, and then descends. Go through a gate and across a field to make for an underpass beneath the A40. Then go over a ladder stile and turn sharp right, keeping a fence on the right. Continue to cross another ladder stile and follow a broad track. Where the path divides, keep along the lower route, just above the fence line, and cross a stile into a field. Continue over two more stiles to pass between two hedges and then cross an attractive wooden bridge. On the right can be seen the remains of the original stone bridge which came to grief some years ago when it was demolished by the Afon Cynrig in flood. The stone house which can be seen on the

right used to be the old Abercynrig Mill.

Follow the lane to the left to reach a junction, and keep straight on. There is a good view from this point, taking in the majestic skyline of the Brecon Beacons.

On reaching a road junction keep straight on to reach a T-junction and turn left. Through the hedge on the other side of the road can be seen Tŷ Mawr pool, a local nature reserve.

At the next junction continue along the B4558 to reach Brynich bridge. This is a four-arched stone bridge crossing the Usk. From its parapets, look down the river to see the neighbouring Brynich aqueduct, which carries the Brecon Canal over the river.

Having crossed the bridge, turn left just past Lock Cottage; go through a gate and follow the canal towpath. The route now passes between two waterways and it is interesting to compare the tranquil waters of the canal on the right with the rushing and excited Usk on the left.

Follow the towpath all the way to pass beneath the A40 and several stone canal bridges, eventually reaching the end of the canal at Brecon basin. Complete the walk by continuing through Brecon, an historic town known in Welsh as Aberhonddu ('the mouth of the Honddu'). Its castle was built by Bernard Newmarch, half-brother of William the Conqueror; the ruins now adjoin the Castle Hotel. Behind it to the north is Brecon Cathedral, which has been described as 'half fortress and half castle'. Other buildings to visit include the Museum of the South Wales Borderers (where relics and mementoes from the Zulu war of 1879 can be seen), Brecknock Museum in the old Shire Hall and the Brecon Beacons National Park Information Centre.

Go down to the river and cross the bridge spanning the Usk, and turn left to reach the starting point.

Corn Du and Pen y Fan

Allow 3 hours

An ascent of the two highest mountains in South Wales is easily made from the A470, which in itself is one of the highest trunk roads in Britain. However, it must be emphasised that inexperienced hill walkers should only tackle this route in good weather, and must be well equipped with suitable footwear, waterproofs, a map and compass.

Start at Pont ar Daf layby on the A470 (SN988199). Go up the track on the left to reach a gate. On the other side, notice on the left the old wartime gun post built to protect this important pass in the event of a German invasion.

Ford the river (quite shallow) and head up the obvious track leading towards the table-like summit of Corn Du. Much work has been carried out on this track by the National Trust and the National Park Service to combat erosion problems. Drainage channels have been cut, and the surface improved with natural materials and stones laid into the bed of the track in a jig-saw fashion. A plaque on the side of the track is reached shortly, informing walkers that the Brecon Beacons were given to the National Trust by the Eagle Star Insurance Company in 1965.

On reaching the col of Bwlch Duwynt follow a track to the left around the side of Corn Du. Directly below in the Taf Fechan Valley are the Upper and Lower Neuadd Reservoirs. These are the highest of all the Beacons reservoirs and the weather reflects this; the average rainfall here is 82in a year.

Stay on the main path at the next junction and head straight up to the col. Then continue to the summit of Pen y Fan. This is the highest peak south of Cader Idris and the highest Old Red Sandstone mountain in Britain. Keep well away from the north side for it is precipitous.

In the event of weather deterioration or poor visibility on reaching the summit of Pen y Fan, walkers with limited navigation experience are advised to retrace their outward route back to Pont ar Daf and to leave the section over Corn Du and Y Gyrn for another day. The Old Red Sandstone of the Brecon Beacons was formed from the sand and mud of a great marine estuary which covered this area in Devonian times, about 300,000,000 years ago. During the Ice Age a huge ice cap covered the mountains and a glacier making its way down to the coast slowly scoured out the landscape, leaving distinctive U-shaped valleys.

Return to the col and ascend the rocky crest of Corn Du. On the summit is a burial cairn which was excavated in recent years. It was found to contain a stone cist, which the experts dated at about 200BC.

Now descend with special care the ridge of Craig Cwm Llwch on the north west end of Corn Du and head for a stone pillar which can be seen in the distance on the ridge above Llyn Cwm Llwch lake. This is the Tommy Jones obelisk, a memorial to a five-year-old who lost his way between Cwmllwch farm and the Login in 1900. Poor little Tommy Jones had a short life, but his memorial provides a useful landmark in misty weather.

Follow a path down into the head of the Taf Fawr Valley below, and continue over Y Gyrn and down to Storey Arms, which is at the highest point of the A470. This building is an outdoor activity centre, taking its name from the old coaching inn which used to stand a few hundred yards to the south.

Follow the grass verge back to the start at Pont ar Daf layby.

SCALE 1:25 000

WALK 11
Waterfall
Country

Allow 2¾ hours

This walk takes in the Mellte Valley in the vicinity of the village of Ystradfellte, visiting Porth yr Ogof cave and a spectacular series of waterfalls of breathtaking beauty.

The Mellte is a good place to spot dippers, known for their extraordinary ability to walk along river beds!

Start from Porth yr Ogof car park (SN928124). Cross the road and follow a signposted footpath which follows the old river bed. At one point it drops down into a hollow where the underground river can be glimpsed on either side of the path. Shortly afterwards the river reappears.

From here the path joins the river bank. Follow this to a footbridge spanning the river. Don't cross it, but take the path to the left, following a waymarked route to reach a point above the Upper Clun-gwyn fall. Descend to a viewing position overlooking the fall. This single leap waterfall is one of a series: the others being the Lower and Middle Clun-gwyn falls.

Continue along the path, crossing a couple of streams and then bear left at the next junction, keeping to the waymarked path which avoids the more dangerous places. Turn left up a side valley and on reaching a fence follow it to the right. This high level path provides tantalising glimpses into the valley of the Mellte. The Mellte is the best known of the head-streams of the River Neath and has a fine sequence of caves and falls, starting at Porth yr Ogof. Lovely limestone woodlands cover the gorges and ¾ mile north-east of Ystradfellte is the ruin of Castell Coch (Red Castle), built of red river boulders and restored in the 19th century.

A junction is reached, where a diagonal path leads down the slope to river level. Turn to the right and go back up the river to reach the Middle Clun-gwyn fall. Then retrace your steps and continue along the river bank following a broad path to reach the third of the Mellte falls, called Sgwd y Pannwr. Look out for dippers, which are sometimes seen on this stretch of the river.

From here the track crosses an area of rocks. Keeping the river on the right, follow a path up over the rocks opposite the falls to reach a plateau where good views may be obtained across the Mellte Valley and south to the Vale of Neath. Continue along the waymarked path and bear left to reach the high level path once more. Turn right and soon the thunder of Sgwd yr Eira fall

on the Hepste River will be heard. On reaching a gap in the trees a good view may be obtained of this impressive fall in the valley far below. A ledge passes behind the fall's curtain of water. Cattle, sheep and ponies were once driven across this ledge by farmers making for the far side of the Hepste River.

A stile is reached on the left. Just beyond this point a path leads down steeply on the right to the waterfall. If you descend to visit the fall, you will need to return to this point.

Go over the stile and into the wood to follow a track winding dimly through the trees, providing a strange contrast to the previous scenery. Leave the plantation to enter a clearing and turn right up a short slope, then go left along a broad track. From here, there are good views across the valley towards the upland heights of Fforest Fawr, which means 'the great forest'. This was originally a royal hunting forest but was farmed out by the Crown after the Middle Ages. It remained Crown land until early in the last century, when 40,000 acres were still unenclosed. At a cost of £16,000, the forest was surveyed and enclosed in 1815-19; and this cost was met with the sale of the forest's better valley land.

On reaching a gate across the track continue past a farm; go over a stile and on beside a fence in front of the farm house. A lane is then joined which is followed back to the starting point. Porth yr Ogof cave may be visited by following a path down from the car park at the start of the walk. It has the largest cave entrance in Wales and the initial chamber can be explored, but deep pools soon bar further progress. The side passages should only be entered by experienced and properly equipped cavers.

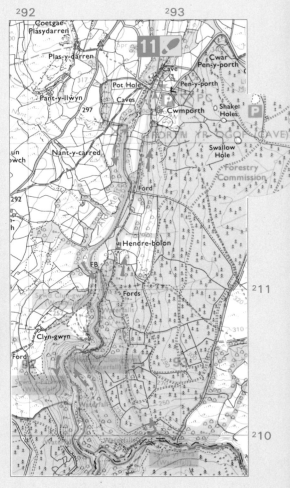

In the Romans' Footsteps

Allow 2½ hours

This route explores the limestone country to the north of Ystradfellte and around the edge of Fforest Fawr. It follows moorland tracks, passes a small Iron Age hill fort and follows a section of Roman Road which was constructed to provide links between a series of camps from Neath to Brecon.

Start from Blaen Llia car park on the Heol Senni to Ystradfellte road (SN927166). Walk up the road and follow it to the left for about ½ mile. On reaching a sharp bend, go straight on to follow a stony track between two stone walls. It becomes a smooth grass path and ascends gently to the ridge above. Go through a gate and keep straight on, ignoring the path on the right. Soon a well-preserved lime kiln below a limestone cliff can be seen to the left. Lime kilns took limestone and burnt it to lime; they are known to have been used in Roman times, and most medieval building contracts included the construction of one or more kilns. They were in common use as recently as the early years of the 19th century.

Pass between two limestone outcrops and continue to a gate set in a wall. The path then crosses the open moorland and forks left to another gate, set in the corner of a stone wall. Do not go through it, but make an elbow turn to the right and head across to a circular fence enclosing a deep shake-hole or swallow-hole. These holes, where streams suddenly disappear underground, are a familiar feature of limestone scenery.

Continue across the moorland to cross a track and reach a stile in a stone wall on the western skyline. Climb past the edge of an Iron Age fort on the crest of the ridge. These hill-top fortifications were built on hills of middling height to act as refuges and cattle-pounds for tribes, clans or family groups, who cultivated the land below or grazed their cattle around them. Some forts were permanently occupied by family groups living in circular houses which were constructed of wood or stone.

Carry on beside a stone wall to pass through a gap in another wall, directly ahead. Descend, keeping right, to an opening in a field boundary. Further on, cross two stiles and join a road. Turn right and follow the road to Blaen-nedd Isaf farm. Enter the farmyard and, at a footpath signpost, turn left and go through a metal gate to the left of a stable. Cross a footbridge, continue up, then turn right to follow the old Roman Road known as Sarn Helen. This ancient route ran from Neath via Coelbren to the Roman fort of Y Gaer, near Brecon. Sarn means causeway and, according to Welsh tradition, the road is named after a beautiful Welsh princess who married the Roman General Magnus Maximus in the 4th century. Alternatively, Sarn Helen could be a corruption of Sarn y Lleon, meaning 'the way of the Legions'; and yet another theory suggests that the name derives from the Welsh *sarn heolen*, meaning 'paved causeway'.

Descend once more into the valley to cross a ford and then follow the Roman Road up the hillside. After heavy rain this ford may be difficult to cross, in which case it may be necessary to return via the outward route. In the distance will be seen a slender standing stone, marked on the map as Maen Madoc. This 9ft stone bears an inscription which is difficult to decipher now, but reads *Dervacus filius Justi ic jacit*; a latin memorial to 'Dervacus, son of Justus. He lies here'.

After passing the standing stone the Roman Road runs through a Forestry Commission plantation and over the site of a Roman camp to join the Ystradfellte road. Turn right here and return to the car park at Blaen Llia.

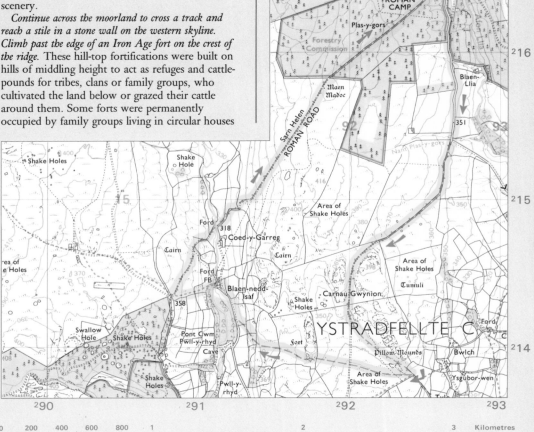

WALK 13
Castle and Cwm

Allow 2¾ hours

Impressive views of Carreg Cennen Castle, standing in solitary splendour on an outlier of Carboniferous limestone above the lovely Cennen Valley, are features of this walk near the western boundary of the Brecon Beacons National Park.

Start from the public car park near Carreg Cennen Castle (SN666194). Follow the lane towards the castle, passing through a farmyard and two kissing gates. Continue along a tarmac path for a short distance directly beneath the castle. At a bend descend to the left, following a broad track across a wooded slope heading down into the Cennen Valley. In the distance it is possible to see the summits of the Carmarthen Fans.

On reaching the floor of the valley, turn right to follow the Afon Cennen. Soon the castle comes back into view ahead, dramatically perched on its limestone crag. According to legend, this castle stands on the site of another fortification, built by Sir Urien, one of King Arthur's knights. The spectacular crag was certainly fortified long before the 13th century, when the present castle was built.

Cross a stile on the left, go down some steps and then on beside the river to cross another stile; go through a gate, and then turn left over a stile to follow a farm lane leading to Hengroffi farm. Walk through the farmyard and pass between the house and a barn to follow a cart track up the hillside. Where the track divides, keep right and, at a junction on a corner, carry straight on. From here there are excellent views of the castle and Cwm Cennen. Carreg Cennen Castle is perhaps the most romantic in Wales, and has a long and fascinating history. It stands on the summit of a 300ft precipice and its Edwardian layout consists of a single ward, curtain walls and towers. One feature of particular interest is a tunnel, extending for 50yds to a well, where the garrison no doubt obtained their water in times of siege.

Go through a gate and across a field, keeping the fence on the right. On the skyline ahead can be seen large stone cairns; these are prehistoric burial sites or memorials, made of rough stones heaped into large piles.

Continue straight on to a gate, where the track becomes more defined, then go through another gate to follow a stone wall. Cross a limestone-scattered landscape to meet a mountain road. Turn right here and, after a short distance, go over a stile on the right. Bear left, passing two large mounds, and make for another stile near two swallow-holes (sometimes referred to as sink-holes or shake-holes). Bear to the left to join a wall. The track now broadens and descends to pass above the source of the River Loughor, issuing from a cave. This has a very difficult entrance, which should only be negotiated by cavers who are experienced and properly equipped. Just above the cave can be seen the remains of an old lime kiln. The Romans built their fort of Leucarum on the River Loughor (Llwchwr) at the point where it turns west to widen into its estuary.

The broad track continues beside the river for a short way and then leaves it to pass through two gates. At the second gate turn right and follow the track down over a stream towards Cwm Cennen. The noble castle is once more dramatically silhouetted against the sky. In a cavern in the cliff below the castle, the Welsh hero Owain Lawgoch (Owain of the Red Hand) is said to be sleeping with 51 comrades, waiting to be called to the aid of his country in a time of great danger.

On reaching Llwyn-bedw farm, don't go through the gate, but turn left and descend through a field to reach a stile. Further on, cross a footbridge over the river. The path then ascends the bank on the other side via three stiles to join the road above. Turn left and follow the road uphill to a junction. Go right and return to the car park.

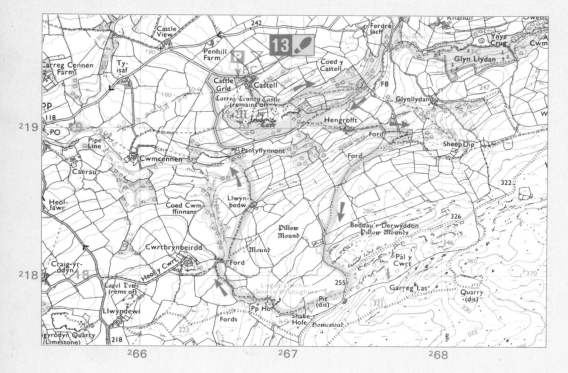

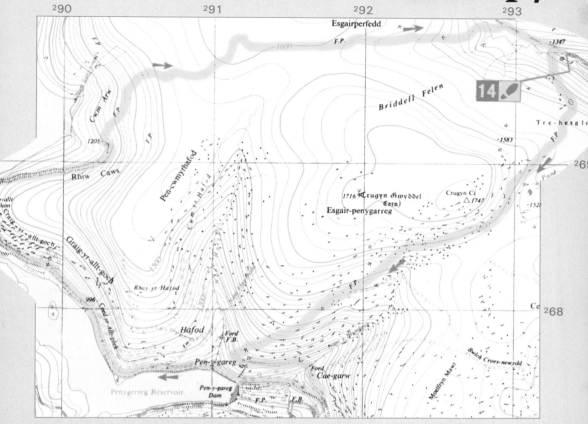

Around the Elan Valley Reservoirs

Allow 4 hours

The area covered by this walk is often referred to as the 'Lake District of Wales'. However, to appreciate the remote and beautiful situation of the Elan Valley reservoirs, the route crosses and re-crosses a mountain ridge, and it must be emphasised that inexperienced walkers should not follow this route in bad weather or poor visibility, for navigation by map and compass may be necessary.

The starting point is on the old coach road from Rhayader to Devil's Bridge. About ¾ mile after passing a waterfall, when travelling from Rhayader, park on the grass verge near where a track leads down to a sheep pen (SN933697). Follow the track down to ford a stream and pass a sheep pen, and climb the hillside. The rutted track provides pleasant walking as it ascends over the southern flanks of Esgair-penygarreg.

On gaining the plateau above, the track becomes less well defined, and it is necessary to make for the right-hand side of the valley, which may be seen below on the left. Follow its line and head for the end of the spur where a stony track will be joined through a gate on the left. This zig-zags down into the valley. Cross a stream on a wooden footbridge and continue through gates, past a farm and on to reach a junction with a road. Turn sharply right and head back towards the Pen-y-garreg

Dam, which may be glimpsed through the trees. It is a dramatic sight when the reservoir is full and the overflowing water cascades over the top of the dam. This is one of three artificial lakes in the Elan Valley which were constructed by the city of Birmingham between 1892 and 1906. A fourth reservoir was constructed in the Claerwen Valley and completed in 1952. The three Elan Valley reservoirs contain a total of 11,000 million gallons of water, and a 72-mile pipeline carries a daily supply of 27 million gallons of water to Birmingham. The Elan and Claerwen reservoirs provide 1,600 acres of fishing water, where it is possible to catch brown trout and American Brook trout, with permission from the Estate Office at Elan Village.

Continue along the track beside the reservoir and go through a gate on the left to follow the bed of an old railway track. This track was built to bring men and materials up the valley when the reservoirs were being constructed.

At one point the track passes through a man-made canyon; it then gently ascends to the Craig-yr-allt-goch dam. Here the water pouring through a line of arches makes a striking sight.

Go past the dam, following a gravel track to enjoy views of the reservoir in the valley below. This bridle path becomes a broad track, snaking up the hillside to reach the plateau above. Below, on a calm day, the reservoir resembles a floating mirror. The large expanse of hill country to the west of the Elan Valley is known as 'the great desert of Wales' and is the largest stretch of wild, uncultivated country in England and Wales.

On reaching a boggy section the track becomes vague and it is necessary to follow the right-hand side of a shallow valley. Head across to the old coach road, which is directly ahead, although hard to see. Then follow the road for a short distance to return to the starting point of the walk.

WALK 15
Whimble and Whinyard Rocks

Dragonflies:
a feature of
Radnor Forest pondlife

Allow 3 hours

Misleadingly, Radnor Forest is a heart-shaped mass of hills. Roughly eight miles wide and six miles deep, they are formed of Silurian limestone. The names of the summits are a strange mixture of Welsh and English.

Park in the main street of New Radnor (SO213608). This is an ancient town situated beneath the hills of Radnor Forest. It was once surrounded by town walls and dominated by a Norman castle, which stood on a large mound and must have loomed very ominously over the little town. Owain Glyndŵr came here in the early years of the 15th century and damaged the fortress so ruthlessly that it was never rebuilt.

Go up the street towards the castle; turn right and then left to follow a lane named Mutton Dingle, which seems to suggest that it is sometimes used by sheep. It is a stiff ascent up the road, passing attractive stone cottages and overlooking a V-shaped valley, which in due course widens into a broad cwm.

At a fork, bear left and follow a cart track beside a fence, on the edge of a forestry plantation. On reaching a gate the gradient eases and the views start to expand. Unfortunately the gradient increases again until the plateau of Mynyddyreithin is reached. Ahead can now be seen the prominent dome known as Whimble.

Follow the track past the base of Whimble and into the next valley where a broad path can be seen continuing past Whinyard Rocks to the top of a pass directly ahead. At the top of the pass go through a gate and follow a fence. On reaching the edge of a wood turn right through a gate and follow a broad path through the bracken to cross the western part of Bache Hill. It is a gentle ascent to the crest of the ridge and this is the highest point on the walk, where an extensive view of the Black Mountains and the Shropshire summits may be enjoyed.

Carry on down the broad, heather-lined track. This provides an enjoyable descent, with beautiful countryside spread out below.

On reaching a gate, go right along a gravel track to another gate, near a large agricultural building beneath the eastern side of Whimble. Now follow a forest road for about 150yds and then take a grass track on the left which descends through a break in the plantations. Further on, cross two forest roads and continue beside a plantation and past a pond. Keep a look out for dragonflies here.

Turn right at the end of the plantation and follow a fence to reach a gate. On the other side, a green lane is joined which descends to the road in Mutton Dingle, leading back to New Radnor.

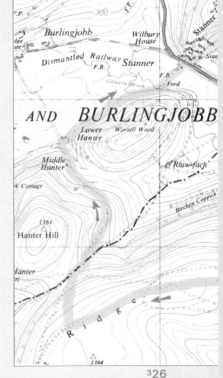

Hergest Ridge and Stanner Rocks

Allow 4 hours

Hergest Ridge is a fine viewpoint on the border of Wales, where the beauty of the surrounding countryside may be fully appreciated. From its heights on a clear day the Clee Hills in Shropshire can be seen, as well as the Malverns in Hereford and Worcester and the Black Mountains and Radnor Hills of Powys.

Park in the square by the Swan Hotel in Kington (SO299567). Kington is a small market town with some good Georgian houses, on the Arrow. Mrs Siddons made her debut in a barn there in the 1770s, and the church contains a 15th-century alabaster tomb of one of the Vaughan family of Hergest. Margaret Vaughan was the wife of Elizabethan adventurer Sir John Hawkins, and founded a grammar school here in 1632.

Go up Church Street, past the church, and follow the A44 for a short way. Turn left up a narrow road signposted Hergest Croft and Offa's Dyke Path. On the left is Hergest Croft, well known for its beautiful woodland gardens of rhododendrons and azaleas. The ghost of a large black dog 'as big as a cow', owned by the Vaughans of Hergest, was said to appear many years ago, when one of the family was going to die. The family's seat was at Hergest Court, a moated manor house built around 1430 near the road to Hay.

Follow the road up the crest of the ridge to reach a gate across the road. From here continue along the ridge to enjoy fine views on either side. To the right is Bradnor Hill, which claims the highest golf course in England (Nantyglo in Wales is higher).

The wide green path follows the centre of the ridge, giving views on the left of the mass of the Black Mountains of Powys and Gwent. A track which encircles the top of the ridge is the old Kington race course, and a slight detour to the right leads to the Whetstone. The Whetstone is a rectangular stone comprised not of the native Ludlow shale, but of a hard igneous rock that must have been deposited here during the glacial period. A local tale claims that every morning at cockcrow it rolls down to the brook to have a drink and then rolls back up the hill again.

Continue past a pool to reach a crossing of tracks. Turn right and descend towards Hanter Hill – a bracken covered mound on the right. *On reaching a col follow the track around the right-hand flank of the hill,* obtaining green and pleasant views down the valley. *Descend to join a track beside a fence and turn left.* Soon, a limestone quarry will be seen ahead on the side of Old Radnor Hill, which marks a change in the geology of this countryside.

Continue past a cottage and on to reach Lower Hanter Farm. Go through a gate and follow a track around the left side of Worsell Wood to reach a footbridge, which crosses the Gilwern Brook beside a ford. Directly ahead are Stanner Rocks, where it was said the Devil had his garden on the summit.

Follow the lane to a gate and turn right by an old railway station and walk with care along the grass verge of the A44. Shortly, an old boundary stone marks the county boundary, and also the point where Wales and England meet.

Go through a gate on the right opposite the turning to Dunfield House, and cross a field and a footbridge; go through a gate and over the old railway track to reach Bestrey Farm. Turn left and continue through the farmyard to follow a lane back to Kington.

A waymarked path follows all 167 miles of Offa's Dyke, and includes the viewpoint of Hergest Ridge

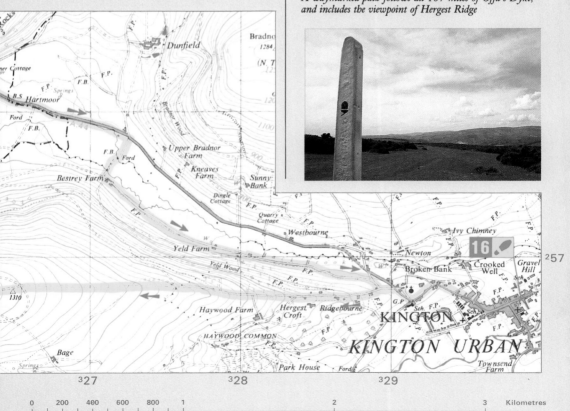

SCALE 1:25 000

Index

Page numbers in bold type indicate main entries.

A

Abbeycwmhir 36, 78
Aberedw 67
Abergavenny 36-7, 41, 75, 78
Abergwesyn 38, 74
Aberystwyth 23, 38-9, 74, 75
activities 74-6
Agen Allwedd cave 45
Alisby's Castle 46
Ammanford 76-7
annual events 80
Ashford Tunnel 37, 109

B

Bache Hill 116
Bethlehem 39
Beulah see Abergwesyn
birdlife 10, 11, 12, 13
birdwatching 74
Black Mountain 53
Black Mountains 15, 39
Blaenafon 22
Bleddfa 66-7
boating 74
Borrow, George 56
Bradnor Hill 117
Brecon 40-1, 75, 77, 98, 110
Brecon Beacons 8, 74, 76
Brecon Beacons National Park 8, 9, 11
Brecon Beacons National Park Mountain Centre 41, 100
Brecon Mountain Railway 23, 69, 78, 109
Bronllys see Talgarth
Bryn Oer Tramroad 109
Builth Wells 24, 26, 42, 74-5, 77, 96
Bwlch 58
Bwlch Nant yr arian Visitor Centre 68, 74

C

Caban-coch Reservoir 48, 94
Caer Caradoc 52
cairns 14-15
Cambrian Factory 59, 79
canals 12, 22, 74
canoeing 74
Capel-y-ffin 42-3
Carmarthen Fans 53
Carreg Cennen Castle 43, 78, 114
Castell Coch 112
Castell Dinas 15-16, 44
Castell Flemish 71
Castell-y-Bere 78
Castellcollen 16, 56
Castell-du 68
castles 78
Cathedral caves 74
Cat's Back (Crib y Garth) 104
cave systems 9, 74
Cefn Coed 76
Cellan 53

Cerrig Duon 15, 60
Cilmeri 42
Cilycwm 44
Claerwen Reservoir 48, 94
Clydach Gorge 21
Clyro 44-5, 96
'Coachman's Cautionary' 56, 98
coal mining 21
Coed Taf Fawr 50
Corn Du 62-3, 111
craft centres 76-7
crafts 32, 34
Craig Cerrig-gleisiad Nature Reserve 45
Craig Goch Reservoir 48, 94
Craig y Castell 76
Craig y Cilau Nature Reserve 45, 107
Craig-y-nos Country Park 45
Craswall 104
Crickhowell 46, 77, 100
Crug Hywel 16, 46
Cwm Cennen 114
Cwm Owen 60
Cwmyoy Leaning Church 46, 102
Cwmystwyth 18, 21, 46-7
Cyfarthfa Castle and Museum 100
Cynghordy 55

D

Dan-yr-Ogof Caves 47, 74, 78
Defynnog 68
Devil's Bridge 9, 39, 48, 56, 94
Devil's Staircase see Abergwesyn
Dial Garreg 105
Dinas Reservoir 68
Dinas Rock 76
Dinas RSPB Reserve 48
Disserth 62
Dolaucothi Mines see Pumsaint
Dryslwyn Castle 55
Dyfi estuary 13
Dynevor Castle 54-5, 74

E

Eisteddfa Gurig 94
eisteddfodau 62
Elan Valley 9, 48, 74, 75, 115
Elan Valley Visitor Centre 78-9
Erwood 96

F

farming 19
Fforest Fawr 60, 112
fishing 11, 75-6
forestry 19

G

Gap Road 16, 50
Garn Goch see Bethlehem
Garwnant Forest Visitor Centre 50, 79
Gelli Aur Country Park 55, 79
geological features 7-9
Giraldus Cambrensis (Gerald of Wales) 51, 54, 56, 58
glaciers 8-9
Glasfynydd Forest 72
golf 74-5
Gospel Pass 50-1
Grwyne Fawr Valley 34, 105
Gwenffrwd and Dinas 74

H

Halfway 56
Harris, Hywel 70, 71, 79
Hay Bluff 50
Hay-on-Wye 51, 96
Henryd Falls 74
Hergest Ridge and Croft 117
hill forts 15-16, 113
historic sites 78

I

industrial archaeology 18, 19-23
information centres 77
Irfon Valley see Abergwesyn

J

Jacob's Ladder 48

K

Kilvert, Francis 42-3, 44-5
Kington 117
Knighton 52, 53

L

lakes 12
Lampeter 52-3
landscape 6-9
limestone quarrying 23
Llanbadarn Fawr 17
Llanddeusant 53
Llanddew 17, 54, 56
Llanddewi-Brefi 17, 54
Llandegfedd Reservoir 75
Llandegley 24
Llandeilo 54-5
Llandovery 41, 55, 56
Llandrindod Wells 23, 24, 25-6, 27, 56-7, 75, 79, 96
Llandybie 23
Llanelwedd 42
Llanfair-ar-y-Bryn 55
Llanfihangel Crucorney 57
Llanfoist 22
Llangammarch Wells 24, 26, 27, 57, 98
Llangattock 58, 74, 76
Llangorse Lake 9, 12, 58, 100
Llangurig 94
Llanidloes church 36
Llanthony Monastery 42-3
Llanthony Priory 58-9, 78, 103
Llanvihangel see Llanfihangel Crucorney
Llanwrtyd-Wells 24, 26, 27, 59, 79, 98
Llanybydder 41
Llowes see Clyro
Llwyn-On Reservoir 75
Llyn Brianne Dam and Reservoir 59, 98
Llyn y Fan Fach 9, 60
Llyn y Fan Fawr 9, 60
Llysdinam Hall 62
Llywel 68
Llywernog Lead and Silver Mining Museum 21, 47, 79, 94
love spoons 49

M

Maen Llia 15, 60
Maen Llwyd 39
Maen Madoc 16, 60, 113

Maen Mawr 60
Maesyronnen Chapel 45
market days 41
Mellte Valley 112
Merthyr Tydfil 75
metal mining 19-21
Monnow Brec Canal 37
Montgomery Castle 78
Morlais Quarry 76
museums 78-9
Myddfai 60
Mynydd Du 105
Mynydd Eppynt 60
Mynydd Illtud 17
Mynydd Llangattock 107
Mynydd Llangorse 108

N

Nant-y-moch Reservoir 68
Nant-y-Mwyn Lead Mine 67
'Nantgwyllt' 48
nature reserves 13, 74
Neuadd Reservoirs 50, 76, 111
New Radnor 61, 116
Newbridge-on-Wye 62
Newtown 33, 75, 77

O

Offa's Dyke 53
Ogof Ffynnon Du 74
Old Gwernyfed Manor House 51
Old Radnor 61
Old Red Standstone 8, 11, 111
outdoor attractions 78-9

P

Painscastle 96
Pant Station 69
paper-making 34
Partrishow 62, 105
Patti, Adelina 22, 44
Pen y Fan 7, 62-3, 111
Pen-y-crug 15, 110
Pen-y-garreg Reservoir 48, 115
Penglais 38
Penwyllt 22
Pinnacle Bay 76
places to visit 78-9

plant life 10, 11, 12
Plynlimon 10
Ponterwyd 56
Pontneddfechan see Porth yr ogof
Pontrhydfendigaid 62, 63
Pontrhydygroes 20, 64
Pontsticill see Taf Fechan Reservoir
Pontymoel 37
Pontypool 75
pony trekking 75
Porth yr ogof 64, 112
pot-holing 74
Presteigne 65
Pumsaint 16, 21, 66, 78

R

Radnor Forest 66-7, 96, 116
railways 20-1, 22, 23
reservoirs 9, 12, 75-6
Rhandirmwyn 19-20, 67, 98
Rhayader 67, 75, 77, 94
Rheidol Power Station and Forest 68
rivers 9, 11-12
rock climbing 76
rural occupations 32-4

S

St David's University College 52-3
Saith Maen 15, 60
Sarn Helen 16, 113
Sennybridge 68, 77, 98
Sgwd yr Eira 9, 65, 112
sheep farming 28-31
Skenfrith 77
Skirrid Fawr 68, 74, 102
Skirrid Inn 57
spa towns 24-7
sports 74-6
standing stones 15
Stanner Rocks 117
stone circles 15
Storey Arms 111
Strata Florida Abbey 17, 78
Sugar Loaf Mountain 68, 74, 106

T

Taf Fechan Reservoir 69

Talgarth 70, 75, 96
Talley Abbey 70-1, 78
Talybont Reservoir 76, 109
tanning industry 33
tramroads 22
travellers in Wales 56
Trecastle 71
Trefeca 71, 79
Tregaron 71, 77
Tregaron Bog 11, 71, 74
Tretower Castle and Court 18, 72, 78, 100
Twm Siôn Catti 67, 98
Twyniau Gwynion quarries 76

U

Upper Wye Valley 67
Usk Reservoir 72, 76

V

Vale of Ewyas (Llanthony Valley) 102
Vale of Rheidol Railway 20-1, 38-9, 48, 79

W

walking 76
Waterfall District 9, 64-5, 112
Welsh history 14-18
Welsh language (glossary) 73
Whetstone 117
Whimble 116
Whinyard Rocks 116
White Castle 78
wildlife 10-13
Wolf's Leap 38
Wolves Newton Model Farm 79
woodland 12-13
wool manufacturing 32-3

Y

Y Gaer 16, 50, 72, 78
Y Pigwn 71
Ysgyryd (Skirrid) Fawr 68, 74, 102
Ystradfellte see Porth yr ogof
Ystraddffin 98

Acknowledgements

The Automobile Association wishes to thank the following photographers, organisations and libraries for their assistance in the compilation of this book. Special thanks are due to the Wales Tourist Board and the Brecon Beacons National Park.

Abergavenny Museum 42 Father Ignatius; *Brecknock Museum* 22 Brecon/Newport Canal, 28 Mr Sidney Hamer, 32/3 Mr Gwyn Price, 37 On the Canal, 44 Adelina Patti; *W Condry* 10 Red Kite, 11 Purple Saxifrage; *A Doughty* 27 Victorian Festival; *International Photobank* 3 Crickhowell; *Llandrindod Wells Museum* 24/5 Municipal Pump Room, 25 Labels, 26 Taking the waters, Brochure, 27 Taking the waters; *C & A Molyneux* 1 High in the Beacons, near Pen y fan; *Monmouth Museum* 17 White Castle; *Nature Photographers Ltd* 11 Raven (M Gore), Rosefoot (R Bush), 12 Goosander (C Palmer), 13 Globeflower (P Sterry), Goldcrest (F Blackburn); *The British Library* 56 Travellers; *Welsh Folk Museum* 19 Timber Felling, 29 Black Welsh Mountain Sheep, Beulah Speckled Faced Sheep, Brecknock Hill Cheviots, Hill Radnor, Clun Ewe & Lamb, 30 Sheep Shearing 1910, Sheep shearing at Neuadd, Sheep washing, 33 Tannery from Rhayader, 34 Tre'r-ddol Clog making, 41 Builth Wells; *Welsh Industrial & Maritime Museum* 19 Cwm Rheidol, 20 Pumsaint, 21 Nant yr arian Lead Mines, 22 Workmen's Train; *Welsh Whisky Company* 40 Lables; *Welsh Tourist Board* 23 Big Pit Mining Museum, 49 Welsh Love Spoons, 53 Stone of Offa's Dyke, 80 Royal National Eisteddfod

The following photographs are from the Automobile Association's Photo Library:

R Eames 44 Clyro Ashbrook House, 44/5 Castell Dinas Hillfort, 56 Llandrindod Wells; *R Johnson* 117 Offa's Dyke Pass; *S & O Mathews* 17 Strata Florida Abbey, 36 Abergavenny Figurehead, 52 Lampeter Church; *C & A Molyneux* Cover Elan Valley Craig Goch Reservoir, 5 Knighton Church, 14/15 Carn Goch, 15 Maen Llia, 16 The Gap Roman Road, 18 Tretower Castle, 18 Tretower Court, 20/1 Cwmystwyth Lead Mines, 28/9 Radnor Forest, 31 View from Hay Bluff, 35 Cilycwm, 36 Abergavenny Castle, Abergavenny St Mary's, 37 Brecon & Mon Canal Lock, 40 River Usk Brecon, 42 Capel-y-ffin, Carreg Cennen Castle, 46 Crickhowell, 47 Dinosaur Park, 48 Carreg Ddu Reservoir, 50/1 View from Hay Bluff, 51 Gospel Pass, Hay-on-Wye, 52 Knighton, 53 Black Mountains, 54/5 Llandeilo, 54 Llandovery, 55 Cynhordy, 57 Llanfihangel Crucorney, Llangammarch Wells, 58/9 Llangasty church Llangorse, 58 Llanthony Priory, 60 Myddfai, 61 New Radnor, 62/3 Pen y Fan, 63 Parrtishow, Doom figure, 64 Ystradfellte, 65 Presteigne, River, 66/7 Welsh Ponies, 68 Taf Fechan Reservoir, 69 Brecon Mountain Railway, 70 Talgarth Brick Barn, 71 Trecastle, 73 Usk Reservoir, Signpost, 76 Vale of Ewyas sign, 78 Brecon Mountain Railway, 79 Llandrindod Wells, 81 Abergwesyn, 106 Sugar Loaf; *C Molyneux* 6/7 Black Mountains, 8 River Tywi, 8/9 Llyn Brianne, 9 Waterfall, River Mellte, 21 Llywernog mines, 38 Aberystwyth University & Castle ruins, 59 Llangorse Lake, 67 Dragon Pottery, 75 Llangorse, 106 Cilau Nature Reserve; *W Voysey* 32 Corn Mill, 33 Tannery, 41 Shepherd's Smock & Hut; *H Williams* 16/17 Y Gaer Roman Fort, 20 Pumsaint Roman Gold Mines, 39 View from Mynydd Llagattock, 40 Zulu Room Borderers Museum, 64/5 Waterfall River Mellte, 68 Viewpoint Sugar Loaf, 72 Y Gaer Roman Fort, 74 Porth yr ogof Caves

Other Ordnance Survey Maps of the Brecon ·Beacons and Mid Wales

How to get there with Routemaster and Routeplanner Maps

Reach the Brecon Beacons and Mid Wales from Liverpool, Stoke-on-Trent, Cardiff and Fishguard using Routemaster Sheet 7. Alternatively, use the Ordnance Survey Great Britain Routeplanner Map which covers the whole of the country on one sheet.

Exploring with Landranger, Holiday and Tourist Maps and Guides

Landranger Series
1¼ inches to one mile or 1:50 000 scale

These maps cover the whole of Britain and are good for local motoring, cycling and walking. Each contains tourist information such as parking, picnic places, viewpoints and public rights of way. Sheets covering the Brecon Beacons and Mid Wales are:

135 Aberystwyth
136 Newtown and Llanidloes
137 Ludlow and Wenlock Edge
146 Lampeter and Llandovery
147 Elan Valley and Builth Wells
148 Presteigne and Hay-on-Wye
149 Hereford and Leominster
159 Swansea and Gower

160 Brecon Beacons
161 Abergavenny and The Black Mountains
170 Vale of Glamorgan and Rhondda
171 Cardiff and Newport
172 Bristol and Bath

Outdoor Leisure Maps
2½ inches to the mile or 1:25 000 scale
Outdoor Leisure Maps cover popular leisure and recreation areas of the country. Packed with information, they are invaluable to the serious walker or climber. A wealth of tourist information is also given including youth hostels, camping and caravan sites, picnic areas, footpaths and viewpoints. Outdoor Leisure Maps 11, 12 and 13 cover the Brecon Beacons and Mid Wales area.

Other titles available in this series are:

Channel Islands	Forest of Dean & Wye Valley	Northumbria	Snowdonia & North Wales
Cornwall	Ireland	North York Moors	South Downs
Cotswolds	Isle of Wight	Peak District	Wessex
Devon & Exmoor	Lake District	Scottish Highlands	Yorkshire Dales
East Anglia	New Forest		